KEEP'N IT SIMPLE

BUSINESS
MANAGEMENT
BUDGETS

*8 Steps to Create, Monitor, and Control
a Business Managerial Budget*

David Hess, PMP

CONTENTS

PREFACE

Keep'n it Simple doesn't mean short on content. The mechanics of developing a Managerial Budget, as well as how to create a monitor and control method for that budget, are subjects covered within this book. Following the steps detailed in this book will not only allow the reader to create a budget, but will also:

- ensure audits go smoothly,
- instill confidence that all important line items have been included and are set correctly,
- establish a Monitoring Plan that prevents over and under examining,
- and form Control Methodologies that quickly analyze and correct issues.

As in all the Keep'n It Simple books, these topics are separated into easy to understand, and easy to implement steps. How-To-Examples guide the reader through exactly how to perform each step.

More **Keep'n It Simple** books can be found on Amazon and linked to from our website.
https://keepnitsimple.weebly.com/

INTRODUCTION

BUDGETS AND BOOKKEEPING

B udgeting is a three-step process.

1. Create the budget: A one-time event.

2. Monitor the budget: An ongoing series of events.

3. Control the budget: A one-time series of events, triggered by a significant deviation in the budget.

To create a budget, it's important to distinguish the differences, as well as the relationships, between a budget and book-keeping. While they are interrelated and complement each other, their roles are different.

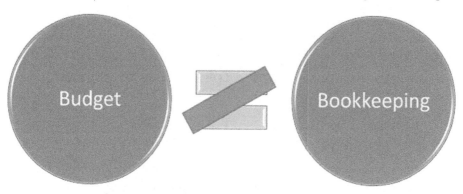

Figure 1: Budgets are not Bookkeeping.

A management budget is a planning tool. It provides an estimate of how much money is needed to run a Company, Business, Department, or Project over a pre-specified period. It serves as a baseline to be used for the control of business performance based upon financial metrics. It provides the basis for monitoring resources such as cash, people, and materials. It also provides a forecast for projecting and for monitoring revenue, sales, expenses, and profits. It's developed in advance of the specified period or project. A budget is a financial roadmap for where its subject needs to go, and a plan for where it needs to be, at any future point in time.

Bookkeeping is a sub-function of the accounting process. Bookkeeping is the entry of financial transactions and actions of a business into a set of journals as they occur. The journals may be in paper format but, today they're more commonly entered and retained using software. How they're entered depends upon which accounting method is being used and then by following rules dictated by GAAP (Generally Accepted Accounting Principles) guidelines. Bookkeeping entries for specified line items are compared against the budgeted values for each as part of the monitoring function. Bookkeeping enables budget performance to be measured and audited against these transactions.

Budget	Bookkeeping
A planning tool developed in advance to project sales, revenues, and or expenses.	The entry of actual financial transactions as they occur.
A roadmap for where you need to go or plan to be.	Entries determined by the rules dictated by the selected accounting method using GAAP guidelines.

Figure 2: Summary of Budget and Bookkeeping Roles.

Historical bookkeeping records are also used to help in the creation of a budget. This practice not only insures a budget line item hasn't been overlooked, but it assists in pre-release analysis to correctly establish budget values, and it enables efficiency and confidence in post-release monitoring. Differences between a current draft budget and historical bookkeeping records are analyzed to ascertain the causes and to determine if modifications are needed to that budget. In this way, bookkeeping is integrally related to a budget. The relationship between them in the creation of a budget, is shown in Figure 3.

First Pass
- Decide what line items to include. Example:
- Sales and revenue for Product A,B,C
- Expenses and costs for production, operations.

Review Past
- Any line item inclusion differences?
- Example: Expenses and costs for assembly, test, manpower have been broken out.

Create
- Enter quantity for each line item based upon current bookkeeping records and future projections

Compare and Revise
- Compare your entries to historic budget entries and adjust the current budget if needed.

Figure 3: Interrelationship between bookkeeping records and creating a budget.

Once a budget is released, actual expenditures and revenues (as reported by bookkeeping) are compared to the budget line item allowances for each. When a significant deviation is found, it is analyzed to determine the cause and to develop actions to control and correct it. These steps make up the Controlling Function of budgets.

CHAPTER 1

STEP 1: CHOOSE AN ACCOUNTING METHOD

There are two basic accounting methods: Cash Basis and Accrual Basis. The difference between them lies in when, and how, transactions are recorded in the bookkeeping journals and, this "when and how" results in significantly different bookkeeping values. Recall, the output of bookkeeping forms the input of a budget. However, bookkeeping outputs also form the values the budget will be audited against. For these reasons, and as shall be shown, the method used to create a budget must be aligned to the bookkeeping accounting method.

Cash Basis Accounting

Cash Basis Accounting is often referred to as Single Entry because only one entry is required for each transaction. When using Cash Basis Accounting, a single journal entry is made when expenses are paid, and another single entry is made when revenue, cash, is received.

One advantage of cash basis accounting is it requires no special training to use or to understand. Transactions are recorded and reconciled in the same way as they're recorded in a personal checkbook ledger. A second advantage of Cash Basis accounting is it easily gives a clear idea of the on-hand status of cash, just as a checkbook ledger provides, at that given moment.

The main disadvantages of using Cash Basis Accounting are it can incorrectly state long-term profitability and, it provides no visibility of future liabilities and their impact on current funds available. This means a manager could spend money now that's needed to cover future expenses.

Accrual Basis Accounting

Accrual Basis Accounting is referred to as Double Entry because two entries are required for each transaction. Every transaction requires a credit entry against one-line item account and a debit entry against another account. Debits increase one account's balance while credits decrease another account's balance. Also, a first set of entries is made when a transaction is incurred, and a second set of entries is made when the cash for that transaction is exchanged.

For example, one entry is made to the debit column of Accounts Receivable on the date when a service is provided, or when goods have been sold, without regard to when the actual cash is received. A corresponding second entry is made at the same time to the credit column of the Revenue Account for this transaction. On the date the company receives the cash for the transaction, an entry is made for the amount in the credit column of Accounts Receivable and another entry is made into the debit column of the Revenue Account.

In this way, Accrual Basis accounting not only records when an expense or revenue is incurred but also, when the corresponding cash exchange has been made. This allows managers to see upcoming expenses and, to ensure money has been set aside to pay them. The ability to "look-ahead" allows managers to proactively keep their budgets and cashflow in control.

The double entry requirement makes record keeping more difficult for non-accountants and, requires some training to understand even if there is a bookkeeper recording the transactions. It also requires additional reports, such as a Statement of Cashflow, to have visibility of cash on-hand because, just like all other accounts, the cash account has a debit and a credit column. Figure 4 provides a quick comparative summary of these two accounting methods.

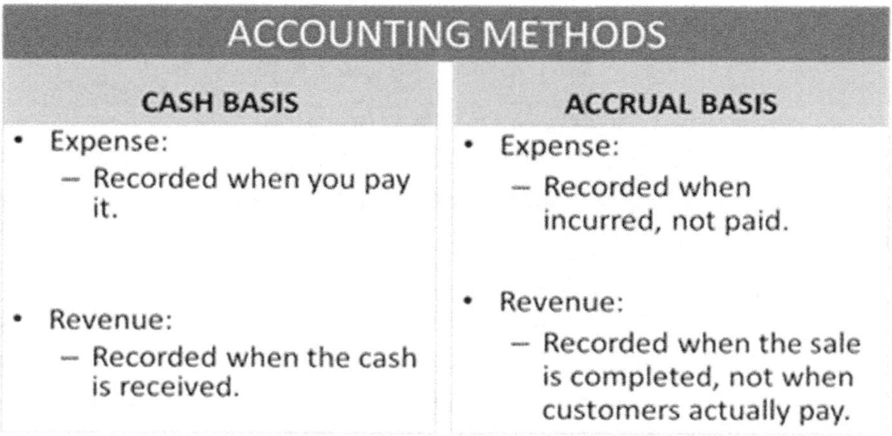

ACCOUNTING METHODS	
CASH BASIS	**ACCRUAL BASIS**

• Expense:
   — Recorded when you pay it.
	• Expense:
	   — Recorded when incurred, not paid.

• Revenue:
   — Recorded when the cash is received.
	• Revenue:
	   — Recorded when the sale is completed, not when customers actually pay.

Figure 4: Cash Basis and Accrual Basis Accounting Comparison.

Example of Accrual Basis versus Cash Basis Accounting.

The significance of these differences is best shown using an example. This example spans a six-month period of transactions using these four assumptions:

1. 10% taxes are due quarterly.
2. Customers pay 60 days after invoicing.
3. Invoice is sent out when the work is complete.
4. Rent is paid monthly but takes 30 days for the landlord to process and clear the transaction.

Table 1 presents a summary of these transactions using Accrual Basis Accounting. It assumes work has been completed and customers have been invoiced as shown.

	Month 1	Month 2	Month 3	Month 4	Month 5	Month 6	total
Revenue	10000	8000	5000	4000	8000	10000	45000
Taxes	-1000	-800	-500	-400	-800	-1000	-4500
Rent	-1000	-1000	-1000	-1000	-1000	-1000	-6000
Profit	8000	6200	3500	2600	6200	8000	34500
Accrued Profit	8000	14200	17700	20300	26500	34500	

Item	Comment
Revenue	Recorded when the work is completed and invoiced even though customers do not pay for 60 days.
Taxes	10% of Revenue, recorded monthly when the revenue is recorded even though they are paid quarterly.
Rent	Recorded monthly and paid monthly.
Profit	Revenue-rent-taxes
Accrued Profit	Past profit + current month's profit.

Table 1: Accrual Basis Transactions.

Using Accrual Basis Accounting,
- Revenue is recorded when it's invoiced.
- Taxes are recorded when the revenue is earned,
- Rent is recorded when it's due.

If this is all that was reviewed, one would assume, based upon the profit line, there's money every month in the account and that there has been a profit in every month.

While the profit assumption is correct, the assumption about cash isn't. A Cashflow Statement, shown in Table 2, is needed to evaluate how much money is available in the bank to spend.

	Month 1	Month 2	Month 3	Month 4	Month 5	Month 6
Revenue	0	0	10000	8000	5000	4000
Taxes	0	0	-2300	0	0	-2200
Rent	0	-1000	-1000	-1000	-1000	-1000
Cash monthly	0	-1000	6700	7000	4000	800
Cash on Hand	0	-1000	5700	12700	16700	17500

Table 2: Accrual Basis Cashflow Statement

Here, cash from revenue is recorded when it's received, and outflows for taxes and rent are recorded when they are withdrawn from the account. In this way, it resembles the monthly bank account reconcile report performed on a personal checking account.

The cash position now appears quite different. At the end of month 1, the balance is zero and in month 2 the cash account is overdrawn by $1,000. The Statement shows a positive balance moving forward from month 3.

Table 3 evaluates the same transactions using Cash Basis Accounting. Here,
- Revenue is recorded when it's received.
- Taxes are recorded when they're paid at the end of

---

the quarter, on the cash received in the quarter,
- Rent is recorded when the check is written.

	Month 1	Month 2	Month 3	Month 4	Month 5	Month 6	total
Revenue	0	0	10000	8000	5000	4000	27000
Taxes	0	0	-1000	0	0	-1700	-2700
Rent	-1000	-1000	-1000	-1000	-1000	-1000	-6000
Assumed Profit	-1000	-1000	8000	7000	4000	1300	18300
Cash on Hand	-1000	-2000	6000	13000	17000	18300	

Item	Comment
Revenue	Recorded when the money is received not when invoiced.
Taxes	Recorded and paid quarterly on the revenue received during the quarter.
Rent	Recorded monthly and paid monthly.
Assumed Profit	Revenue-rent-taxes
Cash on Hand	Past month cash on hand + this month assumed profit

Table 3: Cash Basis Transactions

The difference in the accrued profit is $16,200 less than what was indicated using the Accrual Basis method. The cash position has also changed. The pre-reconcile cash position shown in Table 4 is $18,300. This reflects money received as well as checks written for rent and taxes.

	Month 1	Month 2	Month 3	Month 4	Month 5	Month 6
Revenue	0	0	10000	8000	5000	4000
Taxes	0	0	-1000	0	0	-1700
Rent	-1000	-1000	-1000	-1000	-1000	-1000
Cash monthly	-1000	-1000	8000	7000	4000	1300
Cash on Hand	-1000	-2000	6000	13000	17000	18300

Table 4: Pre-Reconciled Cash Basis Cash Onhand

However, the post reconcile amount shown in Table 5 is $19,300. This difference to the

	Month 1	Month 2	Month 3	Month 4	Month 5	Month 6
Revenue	0	0	10000	8000	5000	4000
Taxes	0	0	-1000	0	0	-1700
Rent	0	-1000	-1000	-1000	-1000	-1000
Cash monthly	0	-1000	8000	7000	4000	1300
Cash on Hand	0	-1000	7000	14000	18000	19300

Table 5: Reconciled Cash Basis Cash Onhand

pre-reconcile amount is due to the 30-day delay from the time the rent check was written and, the time its funds were withdrawn from the account.

The reason the cash on-hand amounts are different between the Cashflow Statement of Table 2 and the Reconciled Statement of Table 5 is directly related to how the two accounting methods record transactions. In this example, under the Accrual Basis method, revenue was recorded when the sale was made and, money was put aside to pay the taxes at that same time. Under the Cash Basis method, the revenue hasn't been recorded until it's received 60 days later. This results in a tax liability of $4,500 in Accrual Basis versus $2,700 in Cash Basis equating to a $1,800 difference.

This cause can be validated by subtracting the Cashflow Statement balance, $17,500, from the Reconciled Cash on-hand $19,300.

Reconciled Cash On-Hand – Cashflow =

$19,300-$17,500 =

$1,800.

While both Cash Basis and Accrual Basis are recognized accounting methods, this example demonstrates the confusion that would result if a managerial budget is created using Cash Basis Accounting but, Finance is using Accrual Basis Accounting to report results. Imagine a scenario where the Manager and the Finance representative are both at the same meeting with Senior Management who asks, "How much cash do you have" or, "What is your profit?" The manager would respond, "My profit is $18,300 and I have $19,300 cash" The Financier, however, would argue, "The profit is $34,500 and there is $17,500 in cash." This confusion is avoided by aligning the method used to create the budget with that used to audit its performance.

Failing to recognize this, I have personally experienced the pain a misalignment in accounting methods causes. We were using a "hybrid" Cash Basis method to report and monitor our Project Budgets, but Finance was using Accrual Basis to report quarterly results. At the end of each quarter, we had to perform the quarterly reconcile. The mismatch in our reported account balances resulted in endless hours of work trying to understand and reconcile the differences. In retrospect, the wise decision would have been to put in the time to train our staff on Accrual Accounting and to then convert our budget method to align to it since that was what Finance was using for the audits. This would have saved time and, resulted in a much less frustrated workforce.

Summary

Most large companies and public corporations use Accrual Basis Accounting not only because it's what is recommended by GAAP, but because it provides a more accurate assessment of revenues and liabilities. A Cashflow Statement is needed when using Accrual Basis Accounting to understand how much cash is actually on-hand. Many smaller businesses use Cash Basis Accounting because its methodology is similar too balancing a personal checkbook. Hence, unlike Accrual Basis, it requires no special training to implement or to use.

Aligning the methodology used to create a Managerial Budget with the method used by the Accounting or Finance Departments is critically important. As demonstrated, failing to do this will result in confusion and time wasted in reconciling the differences. Given this, the first step in creating any budget is to determine which method these departments are using and, to implement it's use, upfront, as the budget is created.

CHAPTER 2

STEP 2: WHAT TYPE OF BUDGET IS NEEDED

Selecting the right type of budget, for the required task, is the next step in creating a budget. Understanding the purpose for the budget will ensure the correct inputs are incorporated, properly analyzed before release, and faultlessly monitored after release.

Cash Budget

A Cash Budget shows the expected cash coming in and going out. This is used for understanding the short-term cash on-hand. At the most basic level, these could be used to budget petty cash; the cash needed to cover those immediate low dollar items such as pens and paper supplies.

At a higher level, a department or business would use a Cash Budget to estimate sales and expenses across a specified period. This estimate would include the delay in time for clients to pay (accounts receivable) and the delay for accounting to disburse funds to pay creditors (accounts payable). Essentially, the company is estimating its Cashflow Statement to ensure it has enough cash on-hand to operate.

Financial Budget

Financial Budgets list receivables and expenditures on a company basis including loans and investments. These also factor in depreciation on capital equipment such as machines and buildings. These are used to estimate projected earnings on those investments.

A Financial Budget should account for the time value of money. The time value of money states that a dollar received today is worth more than one received tomorrow, and a delayed spent dollar is worth more than one spent today. The reason a dollar received earlier is worth more than one received later is because one received earlier can be invested or used. Hence, this interest earning potential must be subtracted from the value of a dollar received later.

The reverse logic applies to spent dollars. A dollar spent thirty days from now earned interest up to that date. Hence, money spent sooner than required lost that interest earning potential. The value of money spent too soon, therefore, is reduced by that earning potential. A practical way for a business to think of, and implement, this is to collect money owed the business as quickly as possible and delay paying interest free money owed by the business as long as possible. A yard service company, for example, requires clients to pay up front but pays for fertilizer they used thirty days later. This strategy allows a business to maximize cash on hand as well as to maximize the ability to put its money to work for them.

Creating a Financial Budget requires a knowledge about interest rates. These are used in the calculations of Future Value and Present Value of loans and investments. Most companies have a set internal interest rate, called a discount rate, they use corporate wide. This rate will likely not be the Prime rate nor, what is advertised at banks. Corporations typically get discounted interest rates and/or base the internal interest rate they use upon some algorithm that factors in these discounts. The corporate discount rate may be difficult to get as most finance departments don't want to share it outside of Senior Management circles.

Top-Down-Budget (TDB)

These are called this because upper management has dictated the bottom line. In this way they are different than most other budgets which are derived from a bottoms-up analysis using estimated expenses and revenue. TDBs, however, still require analysis. Like a household living on a fixed income, the manager may have to make some difficult cuts to stay within the budget. Tips for doing this are presented later in this Chapter, in the section entitled, "Tips When Faced with a Static Budget".

Static Budget

Static Budgets are fixed dollar budgets. The department cannot exceed the dollar amount in a Static Budget. They may be given to a department without any input into their derivation, such as a Top-Down-Budget, or they may have been derived from a contract. Presented here are five contracts that result in a Static Budget.

Contract Driven Budgets

1.   Firm-Fixed-Price Contract (FFP)

An FFP contract results in a Static Budget because the buyer and seller agree upfront to the total cost or, to the cost for each underlying input. The price paid for the service is independent of the actual incurred costs. The seller gets to pocket any additional profits resulting from actual costs being less than the contract agreed price. Likewise, the seller carries the burden of any cost that's higher than agreed upon within the contract.

2.   Cost-Plus-Fee Contract (CPF)

CPF contracts are entered into when the scope is defined, but the underlying costs are not well defined. While the seller is required to estimate final costs within the contract, the seller is reimbursed for all actual costs if they can show they are related to the scoped work. The final fee is the actual costs plus a pre-agreed upon percentage of those actual costs. These are common in general construction projects. Budgets created from CPF contracts must build into them a management reserve in case actual costs exceed estimates.

3.   Cost-Plus-Fixed-Fee Contract (CPFF)

CPFF are similar to CPF contracts. An estimate of final costs is included within the contract but, the seller is reimbursed for all actual costs related to the scoped work. They differ in that the final contract fee is the actual costs plus a pre-agreed upon fee that is independent of actual costs. Once again, building a management reserve into the budget is important.

4.   Fixed-Price-Incentive-Fee Contract (FPIF)

FPIF contracts are a variation of the FFP contract. Like FFP, input costs are agreed upon and preset within the contract. FPIF differ from FFP though in that they have an incentive bonus for meeting or exceeding pre-specified objectives. For example, an interstate road construction shall be completed by October 2020, but a bonus of "X" shall be awarded for every month the project completes before that date. Budgets for these types of contracts have a bottom line that includes the incentive fees. Said differently, the budget assumes the incentive fee will be paid.

5. *Time and Materials Contract (T&M)*

In T&M contracts, the unit rates are preset and agreed to by both the buyer and seller upfront. These contracts are more open ended because the exact quantity of the product to be delivered is not defined; only its unit costs are pre-defined. This is the type of contract often used by attorneys. Client-Attorney contracts will specify the costs for everything from the agreed upon rate per hour to the cost of sending a letter. The final cost upon closure of the case is the summation of all of these. Since the term of a T&M contract is fluid, creating an all inclusive budget is difficult. The best method for creating a budget for T&M contracts is to review historic records or industry norms.

Tips When Faced With A Static Budget

When the Static Budget is Top-Down driven, follow these steps to prevent exceeding that bottom line number.

- **Prioritize expenditures**. This will ensure those critical to the operation are funded.
- **Manage Accounts Receivable and Accounts Payable** closely to ensure they are adhering to the time estimates. This will maintain a positive cash position.
- **Review past budget performance.** Understand where overages occurred, their root causes, and the associated amounts. Then, implement changes that will prevent these from reoccurring in the newly formed budget.
- **Create a management reserve**. This reserve is the "rainy day" fund to cover those unplanned expenditures for unplanned events that will arise. To create this, analyze past budget overages to estimate how much to set aside in this reserve. Creating a reserve fund will help prevent unplanned cuts in other areas by using the reserve fund to cover these unforeseen events.
- **Stay in Scope**. Since costs cannot increase, any overreach of work or specifications beyond what has been contracted (scoped) will result in cost overtures which may not be recuperated.

When the Static Budget is a result from one of the afore mentioned contracts, establish a ceiling price at the beginning. Also, special care needs to be given to Static Budgets spanning across several years. These need to allow for the budget to be adjusted for economic changes such as inflation or currency valuations.

Most companies using Static Budgets will have a Change Control Process that allows a manager to proactively request budget modifications. If such a process isn't in place, create one. Use these only after a thorough analysis has confirmed nothing else can be done to mitigate the situation. Also, make sure corrective actions are in place to insure the underlying cause will not reoccur.

When I was in the military, I personally experienced the downside of a top-down, Static Budget. My work center was given a specific funding for the upcoming year. I wasn't privy to how the amount was derived but, I became acutely aware by my Departmental Officer that we would spend every penny. Each period's ending was met with a flurry of spending on things that we "might" need but, really "weren't" needed at the time. We spent every penny. I was told not doing so would result in funding cuts next year because, we were "over-funded" this year. Ludicrous, I know, but it was how the system operated.

A similar situation can occur in the private sector. When next year's budget is based upon this year's expenditures, managers will do everything within their power to pad the inputs into next year's budget by spending every penny of this year's budget. This is especially true if managers know they will not be rewarded for saving money but will face wrath if they exceed a fixed budget.

Operational Budget

Operational Budgets reflect expected operational revenue and expenses for a specified period. They can also be used to forecast net income and profit. Included in an Operational Budget are the same items as reported on the income statement such as, Cost of Goods Sold and Variable Costs. Included are costs that change with sales such as direct labor, materials, and overhead. Also included are fixed costs that are independent of sales such as, rent and utilities. Furthermore, an Operational Budget should include interest and depreciation from the Financial Budget.

Department Budget

A Department Budget can be bottoms-up or tops-down. It shows all revenue (if any) and expenses for a given department. Some departments, such as Shipping and Receiving, won't have any associated revenue so their budget only reflects the expected expenses.

Compare that to a Sales Department Budget. A sales Department will have revenue from sales and, expenses related to salaries and entertainment.

Project Budget

A Project is a temporary endeavor that creates a unique product, service, or result. A Project Budget follows the same definition. Whether the project has any associated revenue depends upon the definition of the project. If that definition extends to end of life of the product or service, then the Project Budget becomes a Life Cycle Budget.

For example, a company decides to create a project to develop a new product. The project could be scoped to only include the development activities (phase) for that product. Here, the project closes when the product goes to market. In such a scenario, the project has no associated revenue; only expenses. However, the company could choose to define the project to include, not only the development phase, but the production and close-out phases. With such a definition, the Project Budget includes the associated revenues because its scope has been extended to encompass the entire life cycle.

A housing tract is an excellent example of a life-cycle project. It includes many phases. A housing tract project includes the purchase of the land, developing the land, installing the utilities, building the houses, and concludes with the final phase being the sale of the houses. A housing tract project, therefore, includes all associated expenses and revenues.

Life Cycle Budget

Life Cycle Budgets project the sales or, benefit and expenses, across the life of a product or item; from development or purchase to phase out. Items within a Life Cycle Budget include the following phases.

1. **The Research and Development phase** encompasses design, development, prototype fabrication, assembly and test, and supplier start-up.
2. **The Construction phase** includes decisions about whether to build a new site or, to upgrade existing sites or, to outsource the manufacturing to a third party.
3. **The Production phase** for the product includes fabrication, assembly, test, and decisions about inventory.
4. **The Operations phase** includes spare parts, logistics, ongoing maintenance, and utilities.
5. Lastly is the **Phase Out (close out) phase.** It includes costs related to the discontinuance of the product or project. It also includes costs associated with any residuals such as remaining inventory.

Summary

When asked to create a budget, start by asking, "What is the intended purpose of the budget" followed by, "What are the over/under boundaries?" Knowing the intended purpose of the budget helps to not only incorporate all the right inputs but, to perform the correct analysis. Knowing the budgetary boundaries allows for the establishment of an appropriate monitor and control methodology.

Since budgets are made in advance, they rarely end exactly as forecasted. Securing a pre-agreement of the over/under performance boundaries helps establish how tightly the budget needs to be monitored. It's foolish thinking a budget will end exactly as forecasted. Unforeseen events will occur that can cause it to be over budget. These can be mitigated by incorporating a management reserve. It's just as foolish to equate being under budget with having done a good job. Performing significantly under budget means the company reserved funds for that budget that could have generated returns by being allocated or invested elsewhere.

CHAPTER 3

STEP 3: ANALYZE THE BUDGET BEFORE ITS RELEASE

After creating a budget, analyze it before its release as finalized. For budgets without revenues, only expenses, pre-release analysis is limited to a review of historical data from past budgets, their underlying assumptions, their deviations, and steps that could have prevented these deviations. Statistics should be used to quantify past performance and to enable factoring this into creating the new budget. How to do this is discussed in Chapter 5, Statistics Review section.

For budgets with revenues and expenses, pre-release analysis includes not only the afore mentioned historic analysis, but may also include analyses of Breakeven, % Profit Margin, Lifecycle Cost, Payback, and Net Present Value. As will become apparent, not all are applicable for every type of budget. What analysis is required depends upon the purpose and scope of the budget.

Breakeven Analysis

A breakeven analysis is performed to make sure expected revenue will exceed anticipated expenses. At a minimum, breakeven analysis provides the point where revenue equals expenses. There are two ways to find the breakeven point. The first is to calculate it manually. The second is to graph expenses and revenue on the Y axis versus units sold on the X axis.

Manual Calculation
The steps to calculate breakeven manually are as follows:

1. **Determine fixed costs**. This is the cost at zero volume. These are costs that are always present regardless of sales. They aren't dependent upon sales. Fixed costs include things such as rent, taxes, and insurance.
2. **Determine variable costs per unit produced.** These are costs that vary with sales, such as material and labor. These are dependent upon sales volume.
3. **Determine the Contribution Margin**. This is the Product Selling Price (or Revenue) – the Total variable Costs per unit.
4. **Determine the number of units needed to be produced for revenue to equal fixed costs**. The units needed to breakeven are calculated by dividing Contribution Margin, found in step 3, into the Fixed Cost that was derived in step 1.
5. **Calculate the Breakeven dollars** by multiplying the Breakeven units by the Price/Unit.

Example for Manually Calculating Breakeven
Assume project expenses are as shown in Table 6.

Units	Revenue k$	Total Expenses k$
0	$0	$45
100	$20	$50
200	$40	$55
300	$60	$60
400	$80	$65
500	$100	$70
600	$120	$75

Table 6: Budget revenue and expenses.

1. Determine Fixed costs

   (cost at zero volume) = $45k

2. Determine variable costs per unit. Start by taking the total expenses at 100 units produced and subtracting the total expenses at 100 units.

   $50k-$45k = $5k.

3. To find the unit variable cost, divide the total variable cost by the total units produced.

   $5k / 100 units = $50 per unit

4. Calculate the unit product price. This is found by dividing the total revenue by the total units produced.

$20k / 100 units = $200 per unit.

5. The Contribution margin is found by subtracting the unit variable costs calculated in step 2 from the unit product price.

$200 per unit - $50 per unit = $150 per unit

6. Breakeven units are the fixed cost divided by the contribution margin.

$45k / $150 per unit = 300 units.

7. Breakeven dollars are the Breakeven units multiplied by the price per unit.

*300 units * $200 per unit = $60,000.*

Graphical Breakeven
  Graphical breakeven analysis is best performed using spreadsheet software such as Excel. The step-by-step details for doing this are listed here. Readers already familiar with how to create charts and graphs in Excel should consider skipping forward to step 6 as that's where the analysis of the created graph begins.
  1. Input the values from Table 6 into a spreadsheet program such as Excel. The data sheet should look exactly like Table 6.

2. Using Excel, select all the data in the table by using the left mouse click in the upper left cell with the word "Unit" in it and, while holding down the left mouse button, drag over to the lower right cell with the value "$75 "in it. Then release the left mouse button.

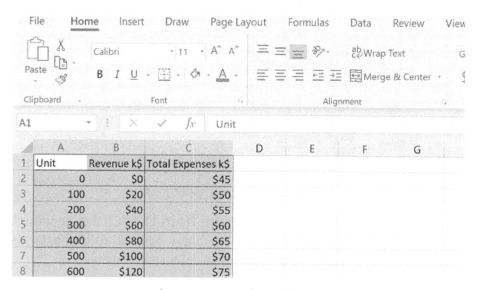

Figure 5: Excel cell highlights.

3. Select the "Insert" tab from the top Excel bar.

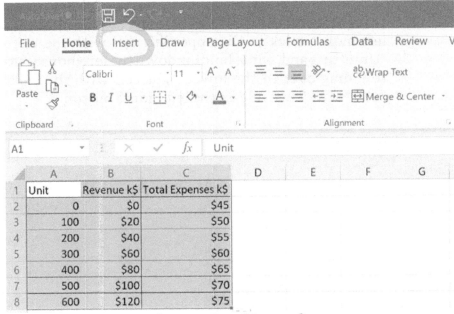

Figure 6: Excel Insert feature.

4. Select the dropdown menu from the "Charts section". This will open another window of available charts already created from the data selected in step 2.

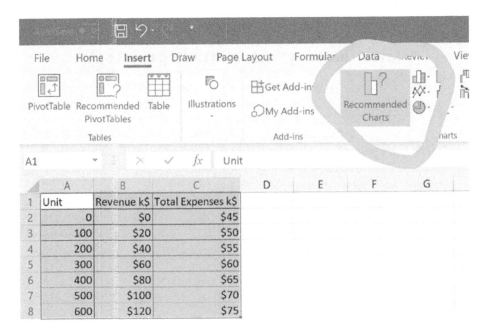

Figure 7: Recommended Charts Feature.

5. Scroll down to the chart that looks like that shown in Figure 8.

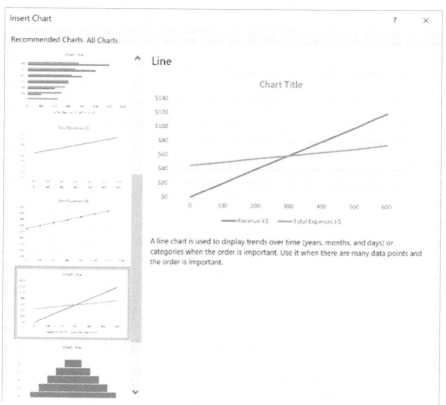

Figure 8: Excel Chart Dropdown Window.

6. The breakeven point is found on the X axis. It's the point where the Revenue line and the Total Expense line cross each other. As shown in Chart 1, it's 300 units.

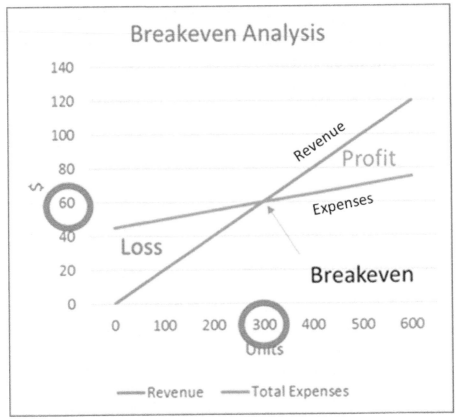

Chart 1: Breakeven Units and Dollars.

7. Breakeven dollars are found from translating this intercept point to the Y axis. It's $60,000.

8. From this example, everything before 300 units is a loss while all units afterwards are a profit.

Profit Margin

Profit margin quantifies overall profitability when revenues exceed expenses. It's calculated by subtracting variable expenses from revenue. This is typically expressed as a ratio as follows:

$$\frac{(Revenue - Variable\ Expenses)}{Revenue}$$

To express this as a percentage, multiply it by 100.

Technically, % profit margin refers to the overall company profit. The correct term for the profitability of an individual product or department is % Contribution Margin. They are, however, calculated in the same way.

Another method for calculating contribution margin was previously presented in the section, Example for Manually Calculating Breakeven. Repeating here it's found as:

$$\frac{(\$200\ per\ unit - \$50\ per\ unit)}{\$200\ per\ unit} = .75$$

Multiply this by 100 to get a percent contribution margin of 75%.

Sometimes when creating a budget, a top down margin that must be met or, to which performance must not fall below, is given as a performance metric. A budget not meeting this value needs to be evaluated to determine how to ether increase the price per unit or, to decrease expenses before its release.

Even if a top down profit margin hasn't been given, it's always a good idea to compare the margin from the budget to some type of baseline. This can provide a "sanity check" as to whether the budgeted line items are within historic or industry norms. That baseline may be past performance, or other products, or perhaps to the industry standard such as may be available at the website http://pages.stern.nyu.edu/~adamodar/ New_Home_Page/datafile/margin.html.

Life Cycle Cost Analysis

Life Cycle Cost Analysis is used to look at the present value of future costs that are projected within a product's life cycle. (Present Value is discussed in more detail a little later in this chapter.) Life Cycle Cost (LCC) is also used to compare total costs of two product life cycles whose life times may differ by starting date, ending date, or duration. Areas included in LCC are:

- Purchase or R&D.
- Construction or upgrades.
- Operations including maintenance, replacement costs, utilities...
- Residual value at the end of its life cycle.

The importance of including all these factors into an LCC analysis is illustrated in Chart 2:

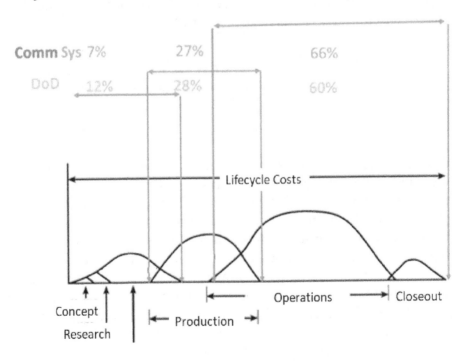

Chart 2: LCC Phases for a DOD and Communication System.

The DOD LCC was found at http://www.dtic.mil/pae/ paeosg02.html . Chart 2 was created by combining this DOD LCC with statistics for a DOD and Communication System derived from (Kerzner, 2003).

Some conclusions drawn from this analysis are:
- ~90% of LCC are post R&D.
- >60 % of the total dollars spent are related to operations and support.
- At the time of R&D complete, 85% of the decisions affecting LCC will have been made.
- At the time of R&D complete there is only a 15% cost reduction opportunity remaining.

However, LCC has its critics. Since it's dependent upon predictions about future expenses and revenues, the accuracy of the LCC is inherently based upon judgement and analogies. Hence a big part of the work in performing an LCC is to question the data and to try to improve the accuracy of these values. This can be accomplished by reviewing historical data from other products.

Another criticism, related to the first one, is that this historical research and estimation requires a lot of resources from many differing departments. Thus, LCC analysis has a high cost associated to perform it.

Lastly, LCC is sensitive to macro and micro economic factors such as inflation, deflation, recession, trade embargos, and changes in interest rates. These, in turn, impact assumptions made about input variables like sales volume, materials costs, and interest rates.

Payback Analysis

Payback analysis is used to determine at what point in time the initial input investment is recovered. It can be used to compare several products or, to see if a project or product is meeting a given target. Any budget not meeting the requirement must be reexamined in areas such as sales quantity, revenue per unit, and costs. In payback analysis, dollars aren't generally brought back to present value, and the only focus is on returning the investment as fast as possible or within a required timeframe.

Payback Analysis Example

Here's an example of how Payback analysis can be used to evaluate three product scenarios shown in Table 7.

Year	Product A	Product B	Product C
1	-$74,000	-$85,000	-$80,000
2	$30,000	$30,000	$30,000
3	$60,000	$44,000	$60,000
4	$70,000	$72,000	$120,000
Sum	$86,000	$71,000	$130,000

Table 7: Payback Analysis.

For this analysis, each product's initial investment is shown in year 1 as a negative value and, for simplicity, it's assumed no positive returns were received within that first year. The goal of Payback analysis is to determine at what future point in time each of these products recoups the initial investment. Figures 10, 11, and 12 demonstrate how payback analysis was performed for each of these three products.

Product A Payback

- $30,000 (Year 2)
- Need $44,000 more
- $60,000 (year 3)/(12 months) = $5,000/month
- $44,000/$5,000 ~ 9 months
- **PAYBACK** : 2 years + 9 months

Return after Payback $86,000
- $5,000/month starting in the 10 month of year 3
- $5,833/month at year 4

Figure 10: Payback Analysis, Product A.

Product B Payback

- $30,000 (Year 2)
- $44,000 (Year 3)
- Need $11,000
- $72,000 (year 4)/(12 months) = $6,000/month
- $11,000/$6,000 = ~2 months
- **PAYBACK : 3** Years + ~2 months

Return After Payback $71,000
- $6,000/month at the 3rd month of year 4

Figure 11: Payback Analysis, Product B.

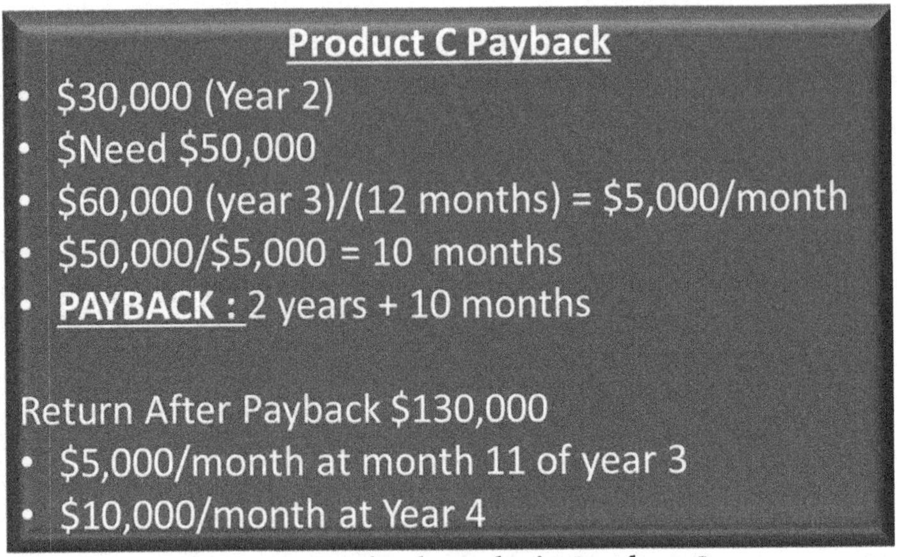

Product C Payback

- $30,000 (Year 2)
- $Need $50,000
- $60,000 (year 3)/(12 months) = $5,000/month
- $50,000/$5,000 = 10 months
- **PAYBACK :** 2 years + 10 months

Return After Payback $130,000
- $5,000/month at month 11 of year 3
- $10,000/month at Year 4

Figure 12: Payback Analysis, Product C.

Using the definition, the preferred product is the one with the shortest payback period. Product A would, therefore, be selected because its payback period is 2 years and 9 months as compared to 3 years and 2 months for Product B and, 2 years and 10 months for Product C.

Though the industry standard definition for payback analysis is to select the one with the shortest payback period, for this example, Product A may not be the right decision. Managers earn their pay when they look at the entire picture and, decide if the rules make sense or, if they apply for their given situation. A savvy manager immediately sees that Product C earns $44k more money for the company, at a greater rate of return, starting only 1 month after Product A. This is a great example of why a manager must look at the big picture.

Present value and Net Present Value

Present value and net present value are used together to evaluate future costs and revenues at today's value. By bringing all costs back to today's value, these analyses provide the ability to compare costs of multiple budgets, across multiple projects or departments, without regard to their individual timeframes.

These analyses require the use of the discount rate (interest rate) used by the company. The discount rate reflects the interest rate of return the money, used to fund the budget, could have earned if it were invested instead of being spent on the budget.

Another input needed for these analyses is the period. This refers to the company policy for the time-period (monthly, quarterly, yearly) for performing such a reconcile.

The difference between Present Value (PV) and Net Present Value (NPV) is that NPV is the summation of all the discounted cash flows back against the initial investment. Here are the equations for each.

$$PV = \frac{FV}{(1+k)^n}$$

PV = present value.
FV = Future value.
K = discount interest rate.
n = the period.

$$NPV = \sum_{t=1}^{n} \left(\frac{FV_t}{(1+k)^t} \right) - II$$

NPV = Net present value.
FV = Future value.
K = discount interest rate.
n = the period.
II = the initial investment.

The use of these two concepts is demonstrated by reevaluating the prior three product example. Assume the reconcile period is a year and the discount interest rate is 5%.

Year	Product A	Product B	Product C
1	-$74,000	-$85,000	-$80,000
2	$30,000	$30,000	$30,000
3	$60,000	$44,000	$60,000
4	$70,000	$72,000	$120,000
Sum	$86,000	$71,000	$130,000

Table 8: Products Without PV or NPV.

Year	Product A	Product B	Product C
1	PV = -$70,477	PV = -$80,952	PV = -$76,190
2	PV = $27,211	PV = $27,211	PV = $27,211
3	PV = $51,830	PV = $38,009	PV = $51,830
4	PV = $57,589	PV = $59,235	PV = $98,724
PV Sum	$136,630	$124,455	$177,765
NPV	$66,153	$43,503	$101,575

Table 9: Products with PV and NPV.

A review between the without and with PV and NPV shows the power of performing these calculations. Each value has significantly decreased as has the actual return of each product.

Rewind to Payback Analysis

Recall, one of the criticisms of payback analysis is that it does not account for the future value of money or possible changes therein; in other words, it does not perform PV or NPV. Table 10 provides a comparison of the prior payback analyses with, and without, PV and NPV applied.

	Product A		Product B		Product C	
	w/o NPV	With NPV	w/o NPV	With NPV	w/o NPV	With NPV
Payback Time	2y 9m	2y 10m	3y 1m	3y 4m	2y 10m	3y 0m
Return after payback	$86,000	$66,153	$71,000	$43,503	$130,000	$101,575

Table 10: Payback analysis incorporating NPV.

Payback Analysis using NPV hasn't changed the decision (following the rules) to select Product A because it still has the shortest payback period. NPV has also not changed the fact that Product C is a better choice because, Product C still makes ~$35,000 more money for the company, at a greater rate of return, than the other products.

The takeaway is that payback analysis should initially be performed without PV and if the results appear close, then repeat it with PV. This recommendation builds upon what has been advocated earlier. Managers need to lead by thinking outside the norms and, make solid recommendations based upon all the data, not just the numbers.

Summary

Prerelease analyses are an important step in creating a budget and reviewing past budgets can yield a wealth of information in that analysis. Reviewing past budgets instills confidence that the current budget values are set correctly. It ensures deviation limits are created at values that prevent both over, as well as under monitoring. It prevents missing a category or line item.

Evaluating past data with statistics is the best way to set new budget values. Using statistics means the "probability" of new budget values coming close to the set values has been incorporated into their settings. Doing so to establish deviation limits means that if they trigger, there is a statistical probability that a significant issue has occurred.

In addition to statistical, historical analyses, prerelease analyses may include a review of breakeven, profit margin, LCC, payback, present value, and net present value. These analyses are not applicable for all budget applications. Most are only applicable when the budget includes both revenues and expenses. Performing these analyses prerelease is a proactive action to verify that, if the actuals perform to the budget, company targets for these will be met. If the analyses indicates the targets are not met, proactive steps can be undertaken to fix related issues and, the budget can be reworked.

CHAPTER 4

STEP 4: WHEN, HOW, AND WHAT TO MONITOR

S ome managers advocate there is little difference between monitoring and controlling but, they differ in scope and purpose. Monitoring lets a manager know if something has deviated while, Controlling is what the manager will do in response to that deviation.

Monitoring is the process and procedures for comparing actuals, as reported by bookkeeping, to the baseline (budget) and highlighting variances or deviations. Monitoring is a continuous process since its function is to watch and detect noteworthy deviations. It starts when the budget is created by determining what to monitor, when to monitor, and how to monitor. It ends when the budget period expires.

Controlling is the resulting series of investigation, analysis, and action taken to determine, and correct, the root cause of a high-lighted deviation. Controlling is a finite process that only occurs if there is a deviation. Its starting point is the flagged deviation and its ending point is the implemented action to address that deviation. Once an action is implemented, the Monitoring function resumes to verify that action has corrected the deviation.

The budget is the baseline plan monitored against reported actuals. (Actuals are what bookkeeping measures.) Budgets can have many input lines and it's unlikely that actuals for each will perfectly match the budget. When working in the Monitoring function, the manager decides which line item to monitor, how to monitor it, and at what level to flag any deviation.

Over monitoring can become a burdensome and unfruitful time sink, result in marginal return, and interfere with a manager's other duties. Ultimately, this ends up appearing like micro-management and reflects poorly upon the manager's management style and leadership abilities

The flip-side of over monitoring is under monitoring. Under monitoring can result in resources needed to make the budget a success being allocated to other activities, misguided priorities, and out of control spending. This too will reflect poorly upon the manager by giving the appearance of an inability to understand priorities.

The question to be answered is, how often should budget line items be monitored? The answer depends upon the type of budget as well as company policy. Always check if the company has a policy regarding the frequency but, before doing so, come in-hand with a recommendation.

When to Monitor

Depending upon the cash position of the department, project, or company, monitoring Cash Flow and Cash On-Hand is typically performed on either a weekly, or monthly basis. Some businesses, especially smaller ones, may even do so daily. Projects, however, are typically measured at completion of certain milestones. Life Cycle Budgets will generally have phase-based budget reviews but, since the time duration of each phase can be long, interim reviews are also typical. Department reviews are generally held quarterly to align with the quarterly corporate exchange reporting cycle, but it isn't unusual to have a monthly review.

How to Monitor

At the highest level, monitor the bottom line overall deviation and react if that deviation exceeds a predetermined limit. However, just because the bottom line is on budget doesn't mean that something isn't occurring under the surface.

Monitoring only the overall deviation could miss important information such as, when one-line item is under budget, but its effect is offset by another line item being over budget. An example where monitoring incorrectly would miss such information would be in a sales budget. Sales volume could be down, but the sales mix has shifted to a more expensive product. In such a case, the budget revenue bottom line is within the high-level deviation limit but, there is important underlying information that will be overlooked. Setting deviation limits for every line item will catch these events but, can require an extended amount of work to implement. Hence, monitoring is best accomplished at the category level.

Monitoring at the category level with deviation limits can be an excellent compromise between bottom-line monitoring and line item monitoring. An example would be if the total budget is within its deviation limit but, an individual transaction within the Cost of Goods Sold (COGS) category has deviated. If the transaction is a large percentage of COGS, the category will flag. If the transaction is a small percentage of the category, the category will not be flagged. In both cases, category monitoring using deviation limits would flag if something needs attention.

What to Monitor

Categories should be established using complimentary pairs. Complimentary pair examples include:

- Profit: Expenses
- Cash Flow: Cash on-hand
- Sales Mix: Revenue
- Assembly Cost: Test Cost

Given a scenario where costs or revenues are over budget and have flagged the category deviation limit, each category forming the pair would be analyzed to determine the cause. The analysis evaluates the underlying line items forming each category to determine which one or more has caused the deviation. This is reviewed in more detail in the next chapter.

Another possible outcome is that something is under budget and has flagged a deviation limit. While almost every manager will react if revenues are under budget, only an experienced manager will react if costs are under budget. A manager should understand why costs are under budget for two reasons.

The first reason is to understand the root cause so that steps can be taken to insure it stays repeatable and, to take advantage of it in future budgets. The second reason to react for an under-budget deviation is to protect the manager's credibility. Having a reputation for consistently coming in under budget will undermine this credibility. With such a reputation, upper management may automatically cut future budget proposals because they are "always padded".

Summary

A manager recognizes that when a budget is created, the company has allocated supporting funds which cannot be used elsewhere. Being under budget means the company has lost an opportunity to have used those "excess" funds to generate other revenue. Being overbudget means the company must defund other opportunities.

Monitoring is the process and procedures for comparing actuals to the budget and highlighting variances or deviations. Monitoring is a continuous process. It starts when the budget is created by determining what to monitor, when to monitor, and how to monitor. It ends when the budget period expires.

A monitoring plan answers questions of "when to monitor", "how to monitor", and "what to monitor". When to monitor can be dictated by company policy, aligned to monthly status updates, aligned to project milestones, or targeted to reconcile for a quarterly statement. Managers must balance the time required to monitor, against the pitfall of monitoring too infrequently. The monitoring frequency should allow enough time to react and to correct a deviation.

Setting deviation limits is an excellent "How To" method. When possible, deviation triggers should be automated to flag when a limit has been exceeded. Spreadsheet software, such as Excel, allows for this functionality.

"What to monitor" depends upon the complexity of the budget, but when budgets get large, monitor at a paired category level using deviation limits. When budgets get large, monitoring every line item will result in time spent evaluating deviations that are not significant to the budget bottom line. Category monitoring allows line items to be combined into groups whose overall contribution to the budget bottom line is significant.

CHAPTER 5A

STEP 5: CREATE A MONITORING METHOD

C hapter 5 is divided into Parts A and B because Project Budgets require unique monitoring methodologies. In Project Budgets, money is integrally linked to budgeted work complete and actual work complete. For this reason, there are unique monitoring methods developed for them. To adequately cover these methods, and since they are not applicable to other types of budgets, they will be covered in Chapter 5, Part B. The material covered in Chapter 5, Part A, are applicable to all types of budgets.

Though each business and budget contain their unique sensitivities, for many types of budgets, monitoring by setting category deviation limits and then evaluating deviations using complimentary paired categories, is a method that prevents under and over monitoring. While a manager can, and should, do this for budgets, there are some additional Monitoring Methods reviewed in this chapter that can bring more insight into budget performance.

Complimentary Pair Monitoring

As discussed in the prior chapter, complimentary pair monitoring includes areas such as:
- Profit: Expenses
- Cash Flow: Cash on-hand
- Sales Mix: Revenue
- Assembly Cost: Test Cost

For the profit and expenses category, if profit is down, evaluate expenses. Specifically, look at variable costs. If variable costs are increasing, look at the make-up of sales; sales mix. If the sales mix hasn't changed, then one or more variable costs line items has increased.

Cashflow is influenced by accounts receivable and accounts payable. These correlate to debt invoice dates, the actual debt payment dates, customers' invoice dates, and their payment dates. Cash on-hand is cash flow's compliment. It's how much money is in the bank account. As pointed out in the accounting methodology discussion, looking at cash on-hand and not upcoming bills at the same time, can lead to spending money that's needed to have on-hand to cover future expenses. Viewing these as a complimentary pair prevents such a scenario from occurring.

The best indicator for the impact of a change in the sales mix is revenue. The best indicator of revenue is Profit Margin or Contribution Margin as applicable. The calculations for both Contribution Margin and Profit Margin were presented in Chapter 3. A flex budget, as described in Chapter 7, can be used to determine and quantify if the variance is due to a change in Sales Volume or, due to a change in Sales Mix.

Assembly and Test costs are another complimentary pair. Here, overall production cost may be in control, but the underlying assembly and test costs may have changed. An example is assembly costs may have increased but, the costs are offset by a decrease in test costs. Monitoring the complimentary pair would catch this.

These are only examples of complimentary pairs which may, or may not, be applicable for a budget. Managers must evaluate their individual budget needs and establish the complimentary pairs that create the best monitory methodology for it.

Determining Deviation Limits

Determining where to set the deviation limit is critical. When a deviation limit is exceeded, action is needed. If set to tightly, "False Triggers" are sent resulting in time being wasted looking at what is a non-significant event. If set to loosely, "True Triggers" are missed resulting in an out of control budget and, a missed opportunity to proactively correct something. Deviation limits are the bridge between Monitoring and Controlling.

Knowing the company or department policy for an allowable budget deviation is always the precursor for setting limits. If one exists, then the easiest method to establish deviation limits is to use the company allowable deviation as the trigger point for each complimentary pair item. Set the same value as the overall budget deviation limit. This overall limit will be the safety net should any of the complimentary pairs deviate, but not enough to trigger their individual limits, yet the sum of which exceeds the overall limit. For example, if the policy is all budgets must fall within 10% of the forecasted value, then that 10% is set for each complimentary pair item and, for the overall budget. A more sophisticated approach is to review past budget, and past category pair performance using statistics.

Statistics

Use statistical methods to evaluate historic performance and, based upon those historic records, to estimate the likelihood the current budget and budget categories will achieve a given target. If some categories in past budgets have performed better than the target, then decide if that past value can also be used in the new budget. Doing so will force repeatability of a good behavior. If a category has historically not met the target, perform an analysis to see if the root cause can be determined and corrected. Implement that correction, and set the deviation limit tighter than the past, ideally no looser than the target limit. Applying statistics can help in determining where to set the budget value and, where to set the deviation limits.

Statistics Review

Entire books are devoted to the topic of statistics. Herein is a brief review of statistical topics needed in the evaluation, and setting, of budget values and budget deviation limits. Readers well versed in this topic are encouraged to skip to Chapter 5B.

Table 11 contains values from nine historical budgets for the category item, Test Costs. Table 11 will be referenced throughout this section on statistics.

Normalized Test Cost Variation
0.055
0
0.1
0.2
0.06
-0.015
0.13
-0.01
0.17

Table 11: Data from nine historical budgets.

Normal and Skewed Distributions

Historical data can follow many distributions but, only two are reviewed in this book; Normal Distributions and, Skewed Distributions.

The term "Normal Distributions" refers to datasets whose majority of values are centered about the average and, around the middle of their total range. Data points taper off from that center point symmetrically. Normally Distributed data follows what is called a Gaussian Distribution. A graph of a Normally Distributed dataset, shown in Graph 1, demonstrates these attributes and, because of them, plots of Normal Distributions resemble a bell.

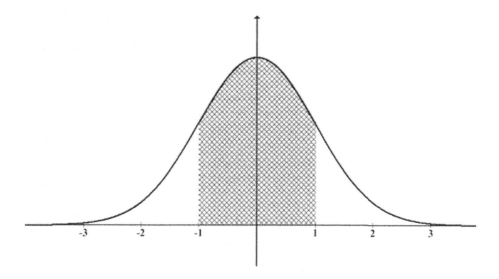

Graph 1: Normally distributed data.

Normal Distributions occur often in nature. When a dataset is normally distributed, terms like average, median, and standard deviation are easily understood, calculated, and applied. In normal distributions, since the data is symmetrically grouped around the center of the range of data, the average equals the median and, the probability of a selected deviation limit is given by the standard deviation. For example, setting a deviation limit at the average plus two standard deviations would allow for 95% of all normal variation.

Skewed data is a type of Non- normal Distribution. In a Skewed Distribution, the data isn't centered about the average nor around the center of the range. It's offset to one of the two sides. It's skewed in one direction. The data from Table 11 is plotted in Graph 2. It's a Non-normal Distribution because most of the data points are to the right side of the peak in the curve.

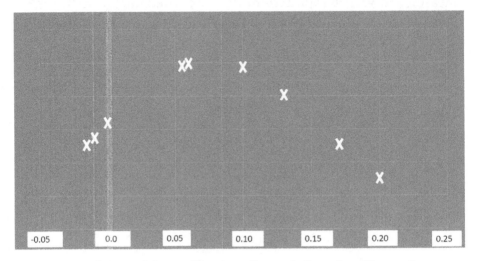

Graph 2: Table 11 dataset plotted showing Skewed
Non-Normal Distribution.

The average of this dataset is 0.08 and the median is 0.06. The average mathematically not equaling the median is the indicator that the dataset isn't normally distributed. Analyzing Non-normally Distributed data requires a different set of calculations than those used for normally distributed datasets.

Normalizing

Normalization of data is a way of giving equal weighting to values that come from different scales. Every budget is going to have a different overall value for each category. For example, in looking at test costs, one budget may have a total budgeted value of $10k with an actual of $11k. Another may have a budget of $30k and an actual of $35k. Choosing to use the over-run values of $1k and $5k isn't the correct method to compare these two budgets because, these values don't represent the portion ("weight") that each represents to their respective total. To account for their "weighting", each number must be normalized by dividing the overrun by its respective total.

For the first budget:

$$\frac{(\$11k - \$10k)}{\$10k} = .1$$

For the second budget:

$$\frac{(\$35k - \$30k)}{\$30k} = .17$$

Before normalization, the second budget's value of $5k appeared to be five times more significant than the first budget's value of $1k. After normalization, however, the significance is only 7%. The data shown in Table 11 has already been normalized.

Sample Size

In statistics, sample size refers to the quantity of data points (past budgets in this case) being used to make an inference about a population (all budgets). The sample size of Table 11 is 9 because it contains nine data points. Statisticians will point out that making assumptions based upon small sample sizes can be prone to error as it may affect how the data is distributed, distort the amount of variability in the data, and thus affect the desired confidence level of the projected value for the new budget. While true, the reality is it's unlikely there will be more than a hand full of past budgets from which to collect the sample size.

Though the sample is small, it still provides useful information, even before applying any statistical analysis. Some useful observations of Table 11 data are:

- Most, six out of nine, of the past budgets completed over target.
- Three of the budgets were below target.
- No budget finished greater than 1% under target.
- Six of the budgets were more than 5% over target.

Before proceeding with any other analysis, a savvy manager would question why these past budgets have performed in this manner.

Average or Mean

The average (mean) of a dataset is derived by adding together all the values and, dividing this total by the quantity of data. When a dataset is Normally Distributed, the average represents the typical (central tendency) value of that dataset. The average of the data in Table 11 is 0.08.

The average can be found using Excel, for a dataset located in cells A2 through A10, by entering the following formula into an adjacent cell:

=AVERAGE(A2:A10)

Median

The median of a dataset is the value at the midpoint of a dataset range distribution. It's derived by sorting the dataset values from least to greatest. The data number that's in the middle of all the dataset numbers is the median. For Non-normally Distributed, skewed data, the median is a better indicator of the central tendency of the dataset than is the average.

- Table 11 dataset sorted in ascending order is:
  -.015, -.01, 0, .055, .06, .1, .13, .17, .2.
- There are nine values in the dataset. The value .06 is the median because it has four data values less than it, and four data values greater than it.
- The Excel formula for median is:

=MEDIAN(A2:A10)

where the range of cells containing the dataset is entered into the parenthesis. Here, the dataset is in cells A2 through A10. The formula returns the value 0.06.

Standard Deviation

The standard deviation (σ) is used to quantify the amount of variation of a Normally Distributed set of data values. The smaller the standard deviation value, the less the dataset values vary from the mean. The calculation for standard deviation can appear daunting but, fortunately, most calculators and spreadsheet software can provide it.

$$\sigma = \sqrt{\frac{\sum(x - ave)^2}{n - 1}}$$

- X=each dataset value.
- Ave=average of the dataset.
- n=quantity of values contained in the dataset.

The standard deviation formula in Excel for a dataset located in cells A2 through A10 is:

=STDEV(A2:A10)

The standard deviation for Table 11 dataset is .08 but, this value should not be used in this case because, as shown, the dataset isn't normally distributed. Standard deviation is only a good indicator of variance when the dataset is normally distributed.

For Normally Distributed data, standard deviation infers the probability where the deviation of a new budget will lie. When normally distributed, 68% of the data distributed about the average will lie within +/- one standard deviation of the mean, 95% will lie within +/- two standard deviations of the average, and 99.7% will be within +/- three standard deviations of the average.

Upper and lower deviation limits should be applied to budgets because, it's as important to know if a budget is significantly under target as it's to know if it's significantly over target. Using +/- a quantity of standard deviations to set these limits results in either 68%, 95%, or 99.7% probability the budget will fall within the limit values. There are methods of deriving other percentages using the standard deviation, but they aren't reviewed here.

However, if standard deviation is used to set only an upper deviation limit, then the entire portion below the average is included (50%) plus, the upper portion of the distribution represented by the number of standard deviations. For example, using 1 (σ) would capture 84% of the data. Using Table 11 values, to capture 84% of the variation, the upper limit would be set att:

$$average+(\sigma) =$$

$$50\% + \tfrac{1}{2}(68\%) = 84\%$$

$$.08 + (.08) = .16$$

Since Table 11 dataset isn't normally distributed, this isn't the correct limit to be used.

Interquartile Range for Non-normal Distributions

The data in a Non-normal Distribution isn't centered about the average. Hence, the average isn't a good indicator of the dataset. Standard deviation also cannot be used because, the average is used in its calculation. The median is a better indicator for a Non-normal Distribution. A measure of variation that uses median in its calculation is interquartile range. This makes it a better indicator of variation for Skewed Datasets.

To manually calculate interquartile range:
1. Find the median of the entire distribution.
2. Find Q1: The median of the dataset below (the lower half of the data) the overall median found in step 1.

3. Find Q3: The median of the dataset above (the upper half of the data) the overall median found in step 1.

Q1 quartile and Q3 quartile can be found using Excel with the respective formulas:

=QUARTILE.EXC(F2:F10,1)
=QUARTILE.EXC(F2:F10,3)

Where the dataset is contained in the range of cells from F2 to F10 and, 1 or 3 represents the desired quartile.

These quartiles divide the dataset into statistically meaningful quarters.

- 25% of the data will lie in the lower quartile below the median.
- 50% of the data will lie below the median
- 75% of the data will lie below the value , 0.15, found as the third quartile.

The interpretation of this means, setting an upper deviation limit trigger at Q3=0.15, would equate to it being set at 15% higher than the set budget value. In doing so, there is a 25% probability of exceeding it.

Percentile

Not as statistically based, yet a valid method, is to base the deviation limit upon a percent limit interpolated within the dataset. The percentile function in Excel returns a percent containing all the data below that value. Its structure is:

=PERCENTILE(F2:F10,0.75)

Once again, the dataset is in cells F2 through F10, and the value returned will be that representing that extrapolated to 75%. The value returned is 0.13. Setting the deviation limit at 13% above the budget target means 25% of budgets would trip the trigger.

Note this isn't the same value returned using the Quartile function. The reason for this is because, the percentile function is using all the data within the defined range including the median value of 0.06. The quartile function, however, doesn't include the 0.06 value. It returns the median of the sub-dataset located above 0.06 for Q3 and below 0.06 for Q1.

Any percentage value can be derived by replacing .75 in the formula, with the desired value; example, entering:

=PERCENTILE(F2:F10,0.9)

returns 0.176, the percentile value at 90%.

Summary of Statistical Terms and Values

Normal Distribution:
- Datasets whose majority of values are centered about the average and, whose data points taper off from that center point symmetrically.

Skewed Distribution:
- The data is offset, not centered, about the average nor around the center of the range.

Sample Size:
- The quantity of data points being used as the dataset.
- Table 11 sample size = 9.

Mean or Average:
- Sum all the dataset values and, divide this summation by the quantity of data.
- Use this for normally distributed datasets.
- Table 11 average = 0.08
- Excel formula: =AVERAGE(range)

Median:
- The value at the midpoint of a dataset range distribution.
- Use this for Non-normally Distributed datasets.
- Table 11 median = 0.06
- Excel formula: =MEDIAN(range)

Standard Deviation (σ):
- Quantifies the amount of variation of a Normally Distributed set of data values.
- One standard deviation = 68% of all data distributed around the average.
- Two standard deviations = 95% of all data distributed around the average.

- Three standard deviations = 99.7% of all data distributed around the average.
- Table 11 standard deviation = 0.08.
- Excel formula: =STDEV(range)

Interquartile Range:

- Quantifies the amount of variation for a Skewed Distribution set of data values.
- Q1: The median of the lower half of the dataset. 25% of the data will be below this.
- Q3: The median of the upper half of the dataset. 75% of the data will be below this.
- Table 11 Q3 = 0.15
- Excel formula: =QUARTILE.EXC(range,Q)

Percentile:

- An interpolated value representing a designated percent containing that amount of the dataset.
- Table 11 percentile .75 = 0.13
- Table 11 Percentile .90 = 0.176
- Excel formula:
  =PERCENTILE(range,%)

Statistics from Table 11 are summarized here in Table 12.

Average	**0.08**
Median	0.06
Standard Deviation(σ)	0.08
1(σ) upper limit	0.16
Interquartile 3	0.15
Percentile 75%	0.13
Percentile 90%	0.176

Table 12: Statistical data derived from Table 11.

CHAPTER 5B

PROJECT MONITORING

P roject Budgets require unique monitoring methodologies because, in them, money is integrally linked to time and resources. Two methods of Project Budget monitoring that factor money with time and resources are Estimate at Completion (EAC) and, Earned Value Management (EVM). A review of EVM is necessary before exploring four methods of calculating EAC.

Earned Value Management (EVM)

EVM is a technique that aggregately monitors costs, work complete, and schedule. By doing so, it provides an estimate of their combined impacts to the budget. It catches hidden costs in scenarios such as current costs being on budget, but the project being behind schedule. Here, there are costs associated with the work related to being behind schedule that are not reflected when only looking at costs that has been incurred. These hidden costs can lead to an Estimate at Completion that's different than what would be calculated without their inclusion. EVM provides the technique for including these factors into the EAC evaluation.

The difficulty in implementing EVM is that it requires knowledge of the time-synced budgeted percent of work complete to the actual work complete. These get derived from the project Work Breakdown Structure (WBS). Doing so generally requires specialized software. Assuming a manager has that software, the power of EVM is best understood using an example.

EVM Example

EVM starts with three measurements:
1. Planned Value (PV).
2. Earned Value (EV).
3. Actual Cost (AC).

Chart 3 shows these plotted for a fictional project.

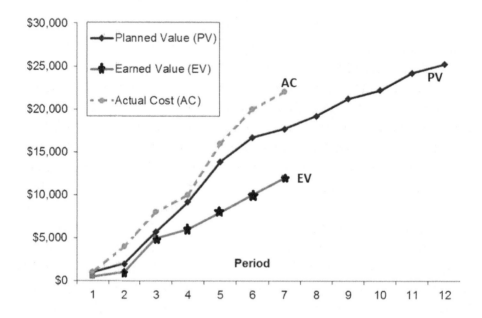

Chart 3: Plots of PV, EV, AC.

- Planned Value (PV) is the budgeted cost for work that should have been completed at a given point. This is the budget.
- Earned Value (EV) is the budget associated with the work that has been completed at that given point.
- Actual Cost (AC) is the actual cost for the work that has been completed at that given point.

In a conventional method used to determine the performance to the budget, subtract the Budgeted Costs (termed PV in EVM methodologies) for the current date from the Actual Costs (AC). Doing so reveals the project is $4.3K over budget.

Amount Currently overbudget =

$AC\text{-}PV =$

$\$22k - \$17.7k =$

$\$4.3k$

Schedule Variance

However, Chart 3 shows EV is less than PV. This means the project is behind schedule because EV represents the budget for the work that has been completed. This Schedule Variance (SV) has costs associated with it related to the work that should have been, but hasn't been, completed. The costs associated with the Schedule Variance (SV) can be determined by subtracting PV from EV; (EV-PV). SV reveals the current cost associated to get the project back on schedule is $5.7k.

$SV = EV\text{-}PV =$

$\$12k - \$17.7k =$

$-\$5.7k$

Cost Variance

To determine the true Project Budget variance to date, add SV + AC to derive a Cost Variance (CV). CV accounts for actual costs and costs associated with a schedule variance.

$$CV = EV\text{-}AC =$$

$$\$12k - \$22k =$$

$$-\$10k$$

In this example, CV is negative indicating the project is behind schedule and over budget. This calculation also shows that the project is currently $10k over budget; more than double what was derived using conventional methodologies.

Schedule Performance Variance

Another useful metric is called Schedule Performance Index (SPI) which is the ratio of EV to PV. SPI shows how efficiently, or inefficiently, the project is using its time as compared to the budget. An SPI of less than 1 indicates inefficiency or, that less work has been completed than was planned. For this project:

$$SPI = EV/PV =$$

$$12/(17.7) =$$

$$.68$$

An SPI of .68 means only 68% of the work that should have been completed to date has actually been completed.

Cost Performance Index

Cost Performance Index (CPI) quantifies the efficiency of the actual costs to the budget. In other words, how efficiently is the actual work being completed. CPI is the ratio of EV to AC.

$CPI = EV / AC =$

$12 / 22 =$

.54

A CPI of less than 1 means there is a cost over-run for the work completed. This project is 54% over cost.

Estimate At Completion *(EAC)*

Estimate at Completion Method 1

The first way to calculate EAC is also the simplest. EAC is the estimated total amount of money that will have been spent on the project. Here, EAC is current Actual Costs (AC) plus remaining Planned Value (PV) where PV is the term used for the budget. Chart 3 shows plotted values for a fictional project. Actual Cost is shown in Chart 3 as $22k. The current budgeted cost is represented by the Planned Value (PV) line. The budgeted PV at the current date is $17.7k. Extracting the PV line to the end of the project provides the Budgeted Costs at Completion (BAC). BAC is $24.2k. EAC, using these three pieces of data, is $28.5k.

$$EAC = AC-PV+BAC=$$

$$\$22k-\$17.7k+\$24.2k =$$

$$\$28.5k$$

This value is compared to the original Budget at Cmpletion (BAC) total to determine if there's a deficit or a surplus. Action is needed if the difference triggers a deviation limit. In this example, the projected is estimated to complete $4.3k over budget.

The issue with calculating the performance to the budget using this first method is it doesn't account for the relationship of costs and actual work performed. It is only looking at costs. The other three methods of estimating EAC account for this by including Earned Value Management (EVM) impacts in their calculations. Unlike the first EAC method, each of the remaining EAC methods includes the impact of work that was supposed to have been, but has not been, completed. Each has its own set of assumptions.

Estimate at Completion Method 2

The second method for calculating EAC assumes the project is going to complete on schedule and, the remaining new work will complete at the budgeted rate. Such an assumption means the work the project is behind on, will get caught up in parallel with the remaining work. This may not be a reality but if it can be done, the EAC is calculated as follows:

$$EAC = AC + BAC - EV =$$

$$\$22k + \$24.2k - \$12k =$$

$$\$34.2k$$

BAC is Budget at Completion and it is $24.2k. The calculated Estimate at Completion of the project using Method 2 is $34.2k; $12.0k over budget.

Estimate at Completion Method 3

The third method of calculating EAC uses a perhaps more realistic assumption; the current rate of work completion will continue. To make this calculation, divide BAC by CPI.

$$EAC = BAC / CPI =$$

$$(24.2) / (.54) =$$

$$\$44.8k$$

Method 3Estimate at Completion for the project is $44.8k; $20.6k over budget.

Estimate at Completion Method 4

The forth method for EAC assumes that the current schedule performance will continue and as such, it uses SPI as a factor in EAC.

$$EAC = AC+(BAC-EV)/(CPI^*SPI) =$$

$$22+(24.2-12)/(.54^*.68) =$$

$$\$55.2k$$

This provides a bleak picture with an Estimate at Completion of $55.2k or, $31k over budget.

EAC Comparison

Each of the four monitoring methods has produced a different result for Estimate at Completion.

1. EAC Method 1
AC-PV+BAC = $28.5k

2. EAC Method 2 =
AC+BAC-EV = $34.2k

3. EAC Method 3 =
BAC/CPI = $44.8k

4. EAC Method 4 =
AC+(BAC-EV) / (CPI*SPI) = $55.2k

Though each method shows a budget overage, the quandary is which one to use. The answer partially lies within if there is an ability to calculate Earned Value. Recall Earned Value (EV) is the budget associated with the work, not just the cost, that has been completed at that given point in time. Every EAC calculation, except #1, requires knowledge of this value and, as stated, deriving it typically requires specialized software. Hence, if EV cannot be calculated, use method 1. If EV can be calculated, then which method to use lies in the assumptions for each. If the project is going to complete on schedule and, the remaining new work will complete at the budgeted rate, then method 2 should be used. Method 3 would be used if the current rate of work will continue but, Method 4 is used if the assumption is that the current schedule performance will continue.

Recall, the Budget At Completion is $24.2k. The over-run values from each of the four EAC methods is as follows:

1. $28.5k - $24.2k = $4.3k
2. $34.2k - $24.2k = $10.0k
3. $44.8k - $24.2K = $20.6k
4. $55.2k - $24.2k = $31.0k

Before accepting such over-run numbers:
- Meet with the team to brainstorm solutions.
- Validate the underlying assumptions.
- Determine if the deliverable can be down scoped to reduce cost and schedule.
- Analyze the causes of the cost overruns and what can be done to avoid or reduce them now or, in the future.
- Determine what is more important; the schedule

or costs. If the schedule is more important, re-sources may need to be added to meet it but recognize, adding resources increases costs.

Regardless of the selected method, still use deviation limits to flag if an over or under budget situation is worth the time to investigate.

Table of EAC and EVM Terminology

Estimate at Completion (EAC):
- The estimated total amount of money that will have been spent when the project completes.
- AC-PV+BAC does not account for the relationship of costs and actual work performed. It doesn't, therefore, require any specialized software to derive it.
- AC+BAC-EV assumes the remaining work will complete at the budgeted rate and the project will complete on schedule.
- BAC / CPI assumes the current rate of completion will continue. The estimated completion date will change accordingly.
- AC+(BAC-EV) / (CPI*SPI) assumes the current schedule performance will continue.

Earned Value Management (EVM):
- A budget monitoring technique that aggregates cost, work complete, and schedule.

Actual Cost (AC):
- The actual cost for the work that has been completed at the given point in time.

Planned Value (PV):
- The budgeted cost for the work that should have been completed at the given point in time.

Earned Value (EV):
- The budget associated with the actual work that has been completed at the given point in time.

Budget at Completion (BAC):
- Total budgeted costs for the project from the starting date to the original completion date.

Schedule variance (SV):

- Costs related to the work that should have, but hasn't, been completed.
- EV-PV

Cost variance (CV):
- Actual costs plus costs associated with a schedule variance.
- SV+AC

Schedule Performance Index (SPI):
- Ratio indicating how efficiently, or inefficiently, the project is using its time as compared to the budget.
- EV / PV

Cost Performance Index (CPI):
- Quantifies the efficiency of actual costs to the budget in terms of how efficiently actual work is being performed.
- EV / AC

Summary

Create a monitoring method that prevents both under, and over, monitoring as both have perils and reflect poorly upon a manager. The use of category pair monitoring strikes a balance between these perils, especially when combined with deviation limits and auto-notification triggers. While examples of category pairs were shown in this chapter, each budget must be analyzed to determine what pairs are best for it. In addition to setting deviation limits on each category, they should also be set on the budget total.

If a company policy does not exist for how much a budget can deviate, use statistics to derive them. Which statistics to use depends upon the distribution of the data. The average and standard deviation can be used when the dataset is normally distributed. Skewed distributions are best evaluated using median and either interquartile range or percentile. The use of spreadsheet software makes the process of creating a budget and deriving deviation limits easier. It also allows for setting auto-notification triggers when actuals are entered.

Project Budgets are integrally linked to time and resources. Therefore, they require unique monitoring methodologies such as Estimate at Completion (EAC) and, Earned Value Management (EVM). One method of calculating EAC that does not require knowledge of the relationship of costs and actual work performed was presented. The three other EAC methods presented, along with EVM, require knowledge of costs integrated with schedule, actual work performed, and planned work performed. Obtaining this requires specialized software but when available, it opens doors to better predict not only project completion dates but, to better predict the EAC.

CHAPTER 6

PUTTING IT ALL TOGETHER

Steps to Create A Budget

The steps to create a budget and, to set deviation limits are as follows:

1. Align the method used to create and monitor the budget, with the method that will be used to reconcile it.
2. Check for company policy regarding allowable under/over limits.
3. Determine which categories to monitor.
4. Get historic budget and actual values and analyze these to see if there are any special underlying causes for deviations.
5. Plot these by budget creation date and look for trends. Perhaps the budgets with the higher variation were from the distant past and, those with less variation were more recent. This would indicate something changed in the method used to create the newer budgets.

6. Determine how the past budget values were derived. For instance, if they were derived by test cost per unit, did all the budgets use the similar cost? Perhaps the lower variation budgets used a higher cost per unit.

7. Determine the underlying assumptions. Amongst other questions ask, did the budgets with a higher deviation assume less retest and less expedite charges?

8. Understand the causes of the deviations. For this example, question if the budgets with the lower deviation built in allowances for retest and expedite charges.

9. Factor this information into the new budget target value. Doing so will reduce the probability of having a similar deviation.

10. After these analyses, reduce the dataset to be used for determining the deviation limits to only include those that are relevant. Here, use only historic data from budgets that correctly factored in retest and expedite fees.

11. Doing these analyses will not only ensure the new budget values have factored in past learning, but that they will also have been factored into the deviation limits.

12. Calculate the average and median.

13. Determine if the dataset is Normal or Non-normally Distributed by plotting the data using software, such as Excel or, by comparing the average and median. Recall, if the median=the average, the dataset is Normally Distributed.

14. For Normally Distributed data, calculate the standard deviation. Use the standard deviation to set the deviation trigger limits.

15. For Non-normally Distributed data, use either the interquartile range, or the percentile, to set the deviation limits.

16. Never set deviation limits that exceed the company allowable limit.

17.   Set deviation limits on each category as well as on the overall budget total.

18.   Set deviation limits to automatically alert when triggered.

Setting Automatic Deviation
Limit Triggers

Just as budgets are best created using spreadsheet software, such as Excel, monitoring methods are also best implemented with some form of software. Using software can provide for automatic notification when a limit is exceeded. In Excel, this is accomplished by using the Conditional Format function. When used, the selected flag will automatically be given when actuals exceed the deviation limits.

Table 13 is an extract from a budget in Excel with conditional formatting activated. Table 13 conditional formatting is set so cells don't change color if limits aren't exceeded. If, however, the entered value is greater than the upper deviation, the cell becomes red. If the actual value is less than the lower limit, the cell turns green. Remember, it's just as important to understand why actuals are under budget as to understand why they are over budget.

Period Budget Test Cost	Lower Deviation limit	Upper Deviation limit	Actual Period 1	Actual Period 2	Actual Period 3
100,000	90,000	113000	105000	113010	89999

Table 13: Budget and Reconcile Extract Using Conditional Formatting to Auto Alert When Deviation Limits are Triggered.

Conditional formatting has been activated using Excel for Table 12 using the following steps.

1. Enter the budget value into cell A1.

2. Enter the lower deviation limit into cell A2.

3. Enter the upper deviation limit into cell A3.

4. Actuals are entered in the cells thereafter.

5. From the toolbar Home tab, select conditional formatting in the toolbar.

6. Highlight (select) the cells where the actuals will be entered.

7. Then, click **Home** > **Conditional Formatting** >

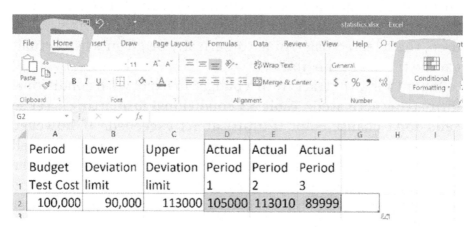

Figure 13: Conditional Format feature in Excel.

8. From the Conditional Format icon, select >**Highlight Cells Rules**

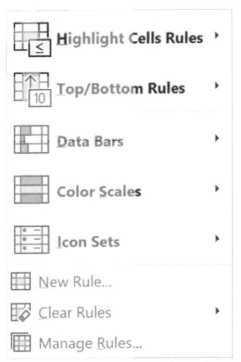

Figure 14: Conditional Format dropdown menu.

9. Then select >Greater Than

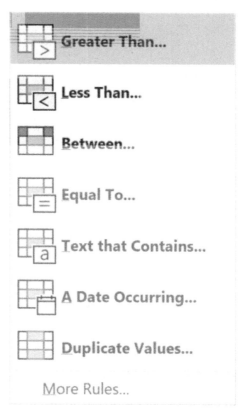

Figure 15: Conditional Format dropdown
menu to select greater than.

10.   Enter the upper deviation limit and the desired color format for the trigger.

Figure 16: Excel window for entering greater than limits.

11. Repeat step 8
12. Select >Less Than

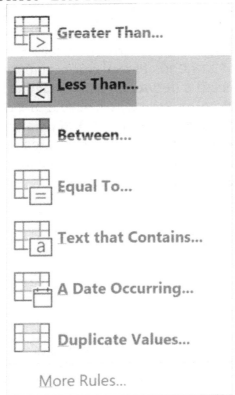

Figure 17: Conditional Format dropdown
menu to select less than.

13. Enter the lower deviation limit and the desired color format for the trigger.

Less Than	? ✕
Format cells that are LESS THAN:	
90000 ↑	with Green Fill with Dark Green Text ⌄
	OK Cancel

Figure 18: Excel window for entering less than limits.

Using Table 11, the budgeted test costs for each period are $100,000. The lower deviation limit, derived from statistical analyses of historical records, is set at $90,000. The upper limit is set at $113,000. Period one actual reconciled value was $105,000. Since it's between the two deviation limits, the cell doesn't change color. Period two actual of $113,010 exceeds the upper deviation limit of $113,000. Therefore, according to the conditional format rule, the cell turns red. Period three actual was $89,999. Since this value is less than the lower deviation limit of $90,000, the cell turns green.

Summary

Now, the budget can be released. Audits will go smoothly because accounting methods have been aligned. There is confidence that all important line items have been included and are set statistically correct. A monitoring plan has been established creating category and statistically determined deviation limits thus preventing over and under monitoring. Lastly, limit monitoring has been automated using software triggers. It's time to move on to the Controlling Function.

CHAPTER 7

STEP 6: ESTABLISH A CONTROL METHOD

Having determined and implemented a monitoring method, the budget has been released so, move to the controlling function. Controlling focuses on analysis and corrective action for a deviation. This Chapter focuses on analysis while Chapter 8 focuses on Corrective action. There are two types of Control analysis that can be used. These are Variance Analysis and, Horizontal Analysis.

Variance Analysis

Variance analysis compares the deviation of actuals, to the budget, at a given point in time.

Analysis of Sales Example

In the example shown in Table 14, the monitoring method has flagged multiple line items in a sales budget for having exceeded deviation limits.

Category	Budget	Actual
Volume	1,000	2,000
Revenue/Sales	100,000	230,000
Material	(10,000)	(30,000)
Labor	(10,000)	(25,000)
Overhead	(20,000)	(40,000)
Profit	60,000	135,000
Difference		75,000

Table 14: Variance Analysis.

An inexperienced manager would be tempted to say, 'Sales are double, and profit is more than double. There is no need for analysis. Let's celebrate!' However, an experienced manager knows differently and digs deeper into the details. Variance Analysis can not only help understand the underlying causes, but also answer if they really were a good thing for the business. One way to perform a variance analysis is to create a Flex Budget.

Flex Budget

A flex budget scales all categories to the actual units. For sales, that's units sold (volume) but, a flex budget can be used for other categories as well. When being used for test costs, the budget would be scaled to actual units tested.

For the sales example, a flex budget determines the variance due to the change in Sales Volume, as well as the variance due to the change in Sales Mix. In this example, the actual units sold were double the budgeted volume, so every item gets doubled. This results in the Flex Budget shown in Table 15.

Category	Budget	Flex Budget	Actual
Volume	1,000	2,000	2,000
Revenue/Sales	100,000	200,000	230,000
Material	(10,000)	(20,000)	(30,000)
Labor	(10,000)	(20,000)	(25,000)
Overhead	(20,000)	(40,000)	(40,000)
Profit	60,000	120,000	135,000
Difference		60,000	75,000

Table 15: Flex Budget.

Using these new values, the variance due to the sales volume mix and, the variance due to a change in the sales mix are calculated.

Sales Volume Variance =

Flex Budget Total – Budget Total=

$120,000-$60,000 =$60,000

Sales Mix Variance =

Actual Total – Flex Budget =

$75,000 - $60,000 =$15,000

These two calculations indicate the $75,000 profit increase can be apportioned as:
- $60,000 due to an increase in the sales volume.
- $15,000 due to a change in the sales mix.

Reviewing only the bottom line total would have overlooked this important information.

Having this information allows further investigation into the details behind the sales mix change. Questions that need to be answered include:
- What products caused the sales mix change?
- Aside from making more revenue and profit, was the change a good thing?

The first question can be answered by reviewing the actual product orders to, the budgeted product orders. (This data isn't shown.) The second question needs some additional calculations that start with a normalization of the values to a per unit basis.

Normalization is performed by dividing each line by the volume.

Budgeted Revenue / Budgeted Volume =

100,000 / 1,000 =100.

This is repeated for every line within the Budget and Actual columns. The results are shown in Table 16.

Category	Budget	Flex Budget	Actual	Budget Normalized	Actual Normalized
Volume	1,000	2,000	2,000	1,000	2000
Revenue/Sales	100,000	200,000	230,000	100	115
Material	(10,000)	(20,000)	(30,000)	-10	-15
Labor	(10,000)	(20,000)	(25,000)	-10	-12.5
Overhead	(20,000)	(40,000)	(40,000)	-20	-20
Profit	60,000	120,000	135,000	60	67.5
Difference		60,000	75,000		

Table 16: Normalization Table.

Normalizing the values provides the following observations:

- Revenue increased $15/unit ($115-$100) or, 15%.

- Material and labor increased $7.50 (15+12.5-10-10) or, 13.75%

Test Cost Example

Assume test costs have triggered the upper deviation limit. Before pulling together a team to perform cause analysis, gather some data to help quantify the variance.

- Compare actual unit test cost to budget unit test cost.
- Has there been a data entry or billing error?
- Are there more units being tested than budgeted?
- If there are multiple test facilities, is the cost from one of those sites higher than the others?
- Was this difference budgeted?
- Did the test mix change? (Perform a flex budget to understand the delta due to the change in the sites versus the quantity of units tested.)
- Is there more retest than expected?

- Is the test time greater than expected and, does the test time overage completely account for the budget overage?
- Are there more expedite fees than were budgeted?

Using Profit Margin

Whether it be sales, or test costs, or any other expenditure, determine if the extra costs were value added by calculating the change in Profit Margin. In the sales example:

Budgeted Profit Margin =

(Revenue-Cost) / Revenue =

60 / 100 = 60%

Actual Profit Margin =

(Revenue-Cost)/Revenue =

(67.5) / 115 = 58.7%

Subtracting the actual profit margin from the budgeted profit indicates the margin delta. This means it cost 1.3% more than budgeted to make that extra $15,000 profit. It also presents another opportunity for managers to earn their pay by answering questions such as:

- Was the decrease in profit margin an acceptable trade-off?
- Can costs be decreased on the more expensive products

David Joseph Hess PMP

that are in the sales mix to increase the profit margin?
- Can sales of the less costly products be pushed to drive up profit margin?

If this was an evaluation of test cost overage due to retest, the change in profit margin due to the cost of retest, would be compared to that for replacing the units with newly manufactured parts. If it's determined it costs less to replace the parts than to retest, the decision might be to discontinue retest until the test methodology of the test program is more mature.

Horizontal Analysis

Horizontal analysis evaluates several periods of variance in a side-by-side method that allows for observation of trends. Two formats that allow for this evaluation are spreadsheets and Graphs. Most readers will be familiar with these techniques. If the reader doesn't recall how to create a graph or chart from a dataset in Excel, review the Graphical Breakeven section in Chapter 3 of this book for the step-by-step details. All can be easily created using spreadsheet software such as Excel.

Often, graphs are better than tables because they provide a pictorial view of trends that allows deviations to be quickly spotted. Though graphs are good for helping to quickly spot a deviation, spreadsheets are better for digging into the details and searching out underlying causes. Here are the advantages and disadvantages of each.

Spreadsheets		Charts and Graphs	
Advantage	Disadvantage	Advantage	Disadvantage
Shows the numbers making up the data set.	Cannot easily spot trends , causes, nor see comparisons.	Good for showing trends and comparisons. Allows for high level visibility of causes.	Can't see the underlying data and the chart can get cluttered if it is added.

Figure 19: Advantage and disadvantages of spreadsheets versus graphs.

There are many types of graphs and charts but, these five are the easiest to create and to help analyze data quickly.

David Joseph Hess PMP

Column Chart

Column Charts are good for showing a comparison of actuals to the budget. Chart 4 is a Column Chart comparing monthly budget totals versus actual totals.

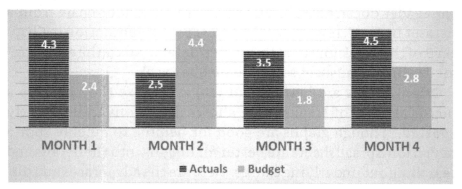

Chart 4: Column Chart.

It shows actuals have consistently exceeded the budget except in month 2. Observing this might initiate further investigation to understand the cause.

Line chart

Line charts, such as Chart 5, are also great for showing comparative trends.

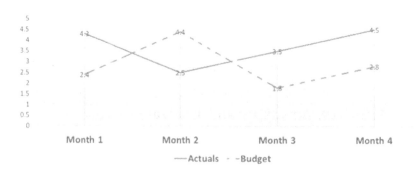

Chart 5: Line Chart.

This chart shows the same data as the prior column chart but in the line format. Hence, the conclusions, and questions, based upon the data would be the same: What was different that caused only month 2 actuals to exceed the budget?

Pie Chart

While pie charts are good for showing an individual category contribution to a total and, for comparison between periods to a total, they don't readily allow for a comparison of these values back to the Budget. Chart 6 is a Pie Chart of monthly contributions to a total.

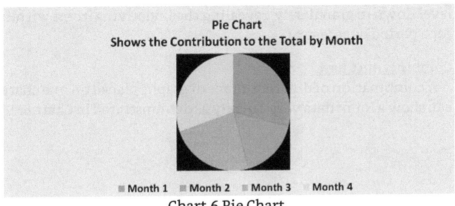

Chart 6 Pie Chart.

A monthly comparison indicates month two was lower than the other periods. The chart does not, however, show if this was forecasted in the budget.

Stack Bar Chart

The same can be said for a Stack Bar Chart such as Chart 7.

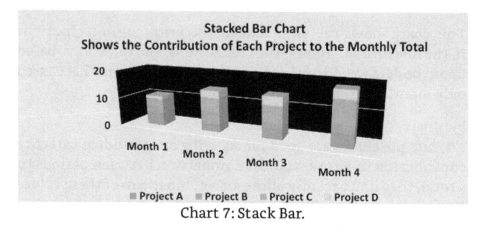

Chart 7: Stack Bar.

The advantage of a Stack Bar Chart over a Pie Chart is it can show a level down in granularity, revealing the underlying items within each period or category.

Combination Chart

A combination of different types of graphs placed on one chart can show a lot of data very quickly as demonstrated in Chart 8.

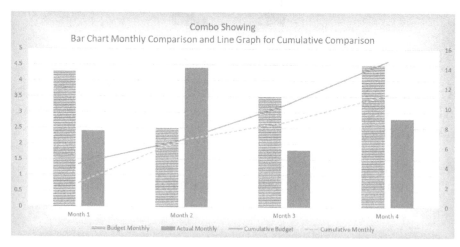

Chart 8: Combination Chart.

Chart 8 reveals the actuals for most months are below budget with month 2 actuals exceeding the budget. One can also observe that the cumulative actuals are below budget.

Summary

Controlling is the resulting series of investigation, analysis, and action taken to determine, and correct, the root cause of a highlighted deviation. Controlling is a finite process that only occurs if there is a deviation. Its starting point is the flagged deviation and its ending point is the implemented action to address that deviation. Once an action is implemented, the Monitoring function resumes to verify that action has corrected the deviation.

A control plan establishes what actions are taken when a deviation occurs. Controlling requires analysis of a deviation and, corrective action for that deviation. This Chapter focused on analysis. The next Chapter focuses on the resulting corrective action. Two types of Control analysis, Variance Analysis and Horizontal Analysis, were reviewed.

A flex budget was presented as a method of variance analysis. A flex budget scales all categories to the actual units. It allows for the determination of variance due to the total as well as variance within the total due to its subcategories. The subcategory of sales is sales mix. A subcategory of test costs would be tester or test facility. The manager must decide the applicable subcategory in order to use a flex budget for variance analysis.

Horizontal analysis provides a visual representation of the variance by displaying trends using charts and graphs. Five different types of charts were reviewed and, their advantages and disadvantages were discussed. Some are best for comparing actuals back to a budget, others are better at comparing subcategory variances across time.

CHAPTER 8

STEP 7: DETERMINE THE CAUSE OF A VARIATION

O nce the analysis has spotted a category that's leading to the deviation, move to finding the root cause. Two popular methods for this are Fishbone and Five Why.

Fishbone (Ishikawa) Diagram

Fishbone (Ishikawa) Diagrams were developed by Kauru Ishikawa in 1982. They are good for capturing the potential causes and sub-causes of a deviation in a visual chart manner. They allow for the identification of all the things that could cause the issue. To use these, begin by identifying (brainstorming) the possible main factors (Causes). Break these down to sub-causes for each factor leg. After identifying the causes and sub-causes, determine how to either validate or, eliminate it as a cause of the issue. (Validation is reviewed in Chapter 9).

Here is a blank Fishbone Diagram. It's easy to see how its name was derived as it looks like a fish skeleton.

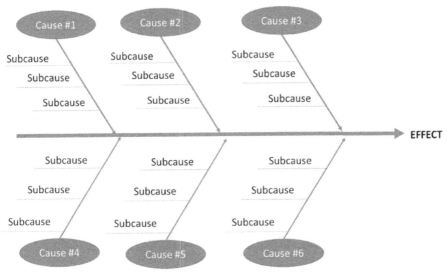

Figure 20: Fishbone Ishikawa Diagram.

Follow this procedure to use it to find possible causes of a deviation.

1. List the deviation in the area labeled "effect" and be specific. Listing the effect as "Costs exceed deviation limits" isn't specific enough. A more specific way of stating this would be, "Variable Costs for Product A of $1M exceed budgeted costs of $700k".

2. Brainstorm the possible cause categories for the deviation such as Quality, test, assembly, logistics...List these as the header for (at the top of) each major branch.
3. For each major branch, brainstorm the possible sub-causes by asking, "Why does this happen". Then list each answer as a new sub-cause.

A great way to do this is to use a large white board or wall. Have the team write the causes and sub -causes on post it notes. The post it notes are placed on the chart in the correct branch.

Fishbone Example

Here is the same diagram completed for high variable costs.

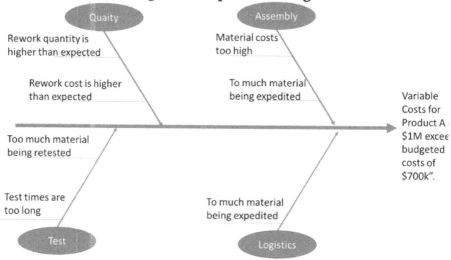

Figure 21: Completed Fishbone Ishikawa Diagram.

Using this diagram, the team investigates each leg to determine if they're the cause, or if a combination of these is the cause.

Five Why Analysis

Five Why Analysis was developed by Toyota. It's useful for exploring cause and effect. It can be used instead of a Fishbone or, when a cause has been identified in the Fishbone, to help analyze that cause further. They are designed to find a root cause. If multiple possible causes are to be explored, a Five Why needs to be completed for each.

Here is a Five Why example found on the WEB at https://open.buffer.com/5-whys-process/ (Seiter, 2018)

1. **"Why did the robot stop?"**
   The circuit has overloaded, causing a fuse to blow.

2. **"Why is the circuit overloaded?"**
   There was insufficient lubrication on the bearings, so they locked up.

3. **"Why was there insufficient lubrication on the bearings?"**
   The oil pump on the robot is not circulating sufficient oil.

4. **"Why is the pump not circulating sufficient oil?"**
   The pump intake is clogged with metal shavings.

5. **"Why is the intake clogged with metal shavings?"**
   Because there is no filter on the pump.

Figure 22: Five Why Example.

The process for performing a Five Why analysis is as follows:

1. List the deviation and, as in the Fishbone process, be specific.
2. Create a list of possible, unrelated causes by asking, "Why did this happen?". Following the same as used in the Fishbone Diagram, these would be:
   a. Quality costs are too high.
   b. Assembly costs are too high.
   c. Test costs are too high.
   d. Logistic costs are too high.

3. Focus on each of these main possible causes, one-by-one, asking," Why did this happen?"
4. Repeat this question for a total of five times or, enough times that the team believes the root cause has been identified.
5. Identify if more data is needed for each "why", what is needed, who will get it, and when they will get it.
6. Repeat for each of the other possible causes.

<u>Five Why Example</u>

A Five Why for test costs being too high might proceed like this.

1. Why are the test costs too high?
The average test program time is 12 seconds versus 7 seconds.

2. Why are the average test program times 12 seconds versus 7 seconds?
The longer average test time is due to 70% of the parts are being retested.

3. Why are 70% of the parts being retested?
70% of the parts are being retested because they fail tests 6 or 10.

4. Why are tests 6 and 10 causing the test time to be 12 seconds instead of 7 seconds?
Tests 6 and 10 have the longest test times and are located near the end of the test program. So, all the prior, lower failing tests, come first.

5. Why are tests 6 and 10 located near the end of the test program?
There is no reason they are at the end of the test program.

With this Five Why, one immediate outcome would be to determine if test 6 and 10 can be moved up to the front of the test program and, if in so doing, would the test time be reduced. An obvious, second follow up Five Why would focus on the root cause, and then correction, of test 6 and 10 failure rates.

Summary

Determining the root cause of a variation is step seven in making a managerial budget. The Fishbone (Ishikawa) Diagram and Five Why Analysis were two methods discussed that guide a team to find the root cause of a deviation.

Ishikawa diagrams are good for capturing the potential causes and sub-causes of a deviation because they are presented in a visual chart manner. They allow for the identification of all the things that could cause the issue.

A Five Why analysis can be used instead of a Fishbone or, to help analyze further a cause identified within the Fishbone. If multiple possible causes need to be explored, a five why is needed for each.

CHAPTER 9

STEP 8: VALIDATE THE CORRECTIVE ACTION

After a cause has been identified, it needs to be validated. Don't make a change without first validating that change in a controlled manner. Validation will insure the change does not cause any unintended, and unforeseen, consequences to other areas. Proceed in the following methodical order.

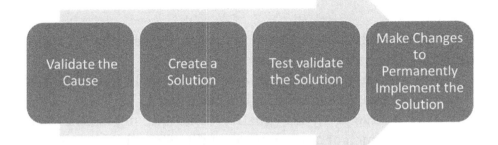

Figure 23: Validation Flow Chart.

Validate the Cause

Validating the cause of a budget deviation may be accomplished by more analysis or, may require a designed experiment. For example, if the deviation is due to a change in the sales mix, analyze which individual product sales have increased and decreased. Create hypotheses of why these have changed and validate them.

For the sales mix example, ask:
- Has there been a change in consumer behavior?
- Is quality of one of the products a factor?
- Is price a factor?

There may be more than one way to solve the problem and, it may require multiple solutions to get the budget back on track.

In the test cost example, perhaps test time has been determined to be too long and is the cause of the overage. Some possible corrective actions might be:
- Could tests with higher fail rates be performed first thus, reducing overall test time on failing parts?
- Could tests that never fail be eliminated or moved to a quality test program that's only performed on a sample of parts instead of all parts?

Perform a paper analysis to determine if these, or other changes, could result in the needed reduction to get back on budget.

Create a Solution

If the sales mix changed because of a perceived quality issue, some possible solutions include:
- Determine how to correct the quality issue and, if doing so maintains the price point.
- Live with the quality issue but determine how much of a price drop would be required to recover sales.
- Correct the quality issue and recover sales temporarily by dropping the price point.

For the test cost example, restructure the test program or test methodology.

Test Validate the Solution

Before making a permanent change, test validate the solution before permanently implementing it. In the sales example, an experiment could be designed to test validate if the believed quality solution corrects the issue. If it's believed lowering the price point will drive sales, a limited time drop in price could be implemented to see if sales recover.

For the test cost example, the test program could be changed at a limited number of test sites and on a limited, but statistically valid, quantity of parts. Actual results would be analyzed against expected results to see if they were achieved. Additional testing on these sample parts might be needed to ensure the changes haven't resulted in any test escapes that would then result in a quality issue. Lastly, the new test program might be rolled out at all test sites for use on limited quantities. This last step would insure none of the sites have an unforeseen issue with the new program. These steps would give confidence that the solution would correct the deviation and not result in any unintended issues.

Implement the Solution

When evaluating the action to take, it's worth mentioning that one option is to not make a change. This decision means the company is accepting the deviation and its impact on the budget. Such a decision may be reached after determining the needed corrective action is more impactful than doing nothing. For example, it costs more to correct the quality issue than to leave it and take the sales/revenue impact.

Lastly, decide if the budget should be reset after having made a change. As is typically the case, there are tradeoffs regardless of the decision. Resetting the budget allows for monitoring what the change was expected to do, versus how it's doing. Resetting the budget means creating a new baseline and a new Budget at Completion. It also entails establishing new deviation limits based upon what the results are expected to be.

Not resetting the budget, keeping the original budget, allows visibility into how much difference the change has made. The Budget at Completion is not changed but new deviation limits may be established that reflect the expectations from the solution. All stakeholders accept the actual Budget at Completion will likely not meet the original Baseline value.Its a good idea, however, to place a note in the budget of the event and correction as a reminder.

Summary

Never implement a proposed solution to correct a root cause of a deviation without first verifying it in a controlled manner. Not only will this validate the solution fixes the issue, it will also insure it does not cause any unintended affects elsewhere.

Once a solution has been validated, two final decisions remain. The first is, whether to implement the solution. The answer lies in the impact the solution has on other factors such as cost, quality, and company reputation to name a few. Sometimes, the right solution is not to make a change.

The second decision is whether to reset the budget or to leave it. Resetting the budget allows for monitoring what the change was expected to do, versus how it's actually doing. Not resetting the budget allows visibility into how much difference the change has made.

BIBLIOGRAPHY

Kerzner, H. (2003). *Project Management, A Systems Approach to Planning, Scheduling,a d Controlling, 8th edition.* Hoboken, New Jersey: John Wiley and Sons.

OFFICE OF THE SECRETARY OF DEFENSE. (1992). *Cost Analysis Improvement Group Operating and Support Cost Estimating Guide.* Retrieved from OFFICE OF THE SECRETARY OF DEFENSE United States of America: http://www.dtic.mil/pae/paeosg02.html#Top

PMI. (2013). *A Guide to the Project Managerment Body of Knowledge (PMBOK Guide), 5th Edition.* Newton Square: Project Management Institute.

Seiter, C. (2018, September 18). *The 5 Whys Process We Use to Understand the Root of Any Problem.* Retrieved from Buffer, Open Blog: https://open.buffer.com/5-whys-process/

ABOUT THE AUTHOR

David Hess is an author, business founder, and business consultant with over 20 years international business and program management experience. He has a BSEE, MSEE, an MBA, and holds certifications as a PMP and an ESL instructor. In addition to his "Keep'n it Simple" books, he posts instructional videos and blogs on YouTube, Linkedin, and his Website.

https://www.youtube.com/channel/
UCr4RxbVVtjmom_ZMD2U6Ebw

www.linkedin.com/in/david-hess-6b795491

http://www.bestconsultingspecialistsinc.com/

Made in the USA
Coppell, TX
14 August 2022

81452151R10066